The Art of Office War

by Simon Drake

To all the people I had the pleasure of working with.

The Art of Office War
1ˢᵗ Edition
Text and images © 2006 Simon Drake

Written, Illustrated and Published by Simon Drake
35 Mollison St, West End, 4101,
Brisbane, Queensland, Australia.

theartofofficewar@simondrake.com

www.simondrake.com
www.theartofofficewar.com

The Art of Office War

Introduction

Early Warrior...

... and Knowledge Warrior

Impressions and Reality

The first impressions of an office are comforting: a warm welcome, an important but not too imposing title, a nice ergonomically adjustable chair and desk conforming to some workplace health and safety specification, and lastly, friendly colleagues. It is a stable and rewarding environment, the fruit of modernity and equality, and all that you need to make an effort and contribute to society is at your fingertips. Be grateful that you are in an office because it's a long way from eking an existence on the hostile savannahs we humans and sabre-tooth tigers used to share, it's healthier than an underground industrial revolution coalmine and in terms of conducting business globally, it's hardly as terrifying as fighting (and maybe dying) for your nation's economic superiority in a war over resources in a savage land.

Over a third of the workforce in the West is employed within the knowledge economy and so they spend their days in the humble office. In relation to everything else this environment is a relaxing place to be, but for all the comfort there are flipsides – it is not exactly a gravy train to an easy life. Beneath the gentle hum of productivity, social chit-chat and civility runs a vicious undercurrent of conduct, competitiveness, reward and status. At stake is your weekly wage, power, and a sense of worth and purpose in a world and time where nothing is certain.

The Road to the Office

The fundamentals of the office are nothing new. Over 100,000 years before we begrudgingly accepted the concept of 'Team Spirit' we were dancing around a freshly slaughtered animal celebrating 'Tribal Survival'. Life was hard, but success actually led to euphoria. We had next to nothing, many of us didn't live long, and those that did adapted to survive. As we evolved, our social networking skills shifted from snarling, biting, banging fists and grunts to hand-shakes, language, and literacy. Now we have advanced so far that we have pre-nuptial contracts, resolutions on non-existent weapons of mass destruction, and climate change treaties that are full of hot air. The art of the profitable allegiance, extracting the most from our enemies, and grouping together in times of need, are all second nature to us. In addition, there are laws, codes, and an established order in our society that keeps us safe from the savage and chaotic ways of life and nature that we think are safely in the past. All along the goal was plain and simple: survive and advance – and we did it. Congratulations.

Now that we are safely in the future, fed and employed, and marvelling (or complaining) at civilisation's ingenuity we have time to take a good look at how we got here and the system we have established. The current system is a life sentence (usually referred to as a career), and like any system that serves so many, it is not without faults. Someone profits, someone loses, wheels fall off, things go pear-shaped, and people get left behind. Hopefully, the worst that can happen is that you fall from one system and bounce up and down in another – the welfare net. Again, we must learn to adapt to survive and prosper. Life has always been a constant struggle, only now it's played out in the office, and even though a time of luxury seems to have arrived, time doesn't stand still.

Think of the impact of technology. In the last century, our minds have advanced with the take-up of new inventions designed to aid society, the workplace, and enhance our leisure time: telephones, facsimiles, computers, email, instant messaging, the conference call that links multiple time-zones, new stimulating content: film, television, internet, and computer games, which are all increasingly complex. Today we are supposedly sharper, able to instantly grasp distinct threads of information that are part of a wider all-connected-web, formulate a succinct answer that somehow aids an overall strategy, and deliver it by eight AM tomorrow. We're the same species, but the speed at which we're operating is accelerating. Now if you have got your head around all the new technologies and think you're sharp enough to take on more, check out your younger competition. Is technology making things easier, or is life universally competitive as nature intended it?

Not to be forgotten in the package of life and work is chaos – creator and destroyer. You may be a high flying executive soaring with the eagles, or embedded like a lazy tick sucking a nice income from your employer, but if the economy has a hiccup then you could be thrown out onto the street staring down the barrel of unemployed frustration, endless job searching, mind draining re-training, and anything else irritating. Your job today determines your job tomorrow, and regardless of whether you perform like a star or a mindless robot, if the shit hits the fan you'll be taken to the cleaners. Your only hope in the office is to evolve, keep ahead of the new blood, be open to change, pray everything turns out all right, and hammer away every day while chaos patiently circles above you.

So how to get ahead and stay ahead in the office? The pen is sharper than the sword and the game is really the same as it ever was, but the pace and environment are changing. There are guides to help you build confidence and expand your mind, but there are also brutal unwritten truths that are too 'un-civil' to be circulated for the benefit of all in the office. But before you set out to learn anything you also have to know what you want.

The Prize

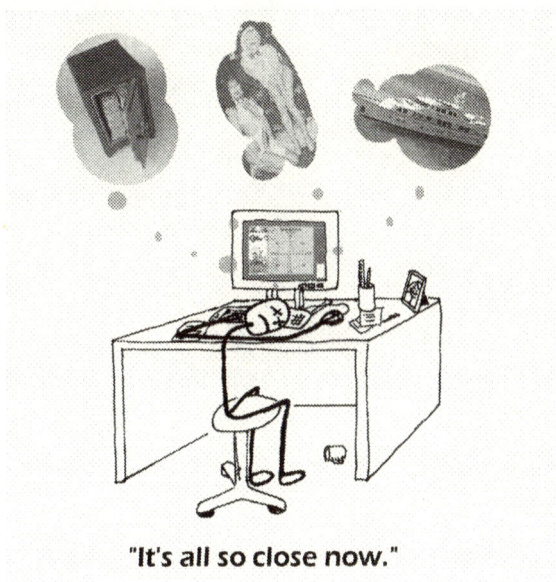

"It's all so close now."

What's on Offer?

Without getting religious and asking God, or getting too serious and having to pay a life coach for advice, ask yourself: what do you really want? Is it the new car, a home of your own, a stake in the world, or simply respect, pride, and a sense of purpose? In the office people get lost for weeks, decades and whole careers, simply earning money, filling time, waiting for guidance or inspiration to tickle their idle buttocks into action. Forget all that. People that move on do so because they see the prize, and before you can say 'Hey! Where are you going?' they're halfway to having their hands on it.

Mostly it's money, cold hard cash in your hand (like when you were paid in the Time Before Electronic Banking). But cash, however you get it, doesn't magically appear either, and the means by which it is earned in the office becomes part of the prize itself.

Responsibility & Accountability of Resources

Responsibility inspires people. It doesn't come for free and it gives meaning to their working lives; a chance to use more than just one percent of their brain power; a taste of professional excitement; and at the high end, the power to hire, fire, and write cheques. They are committed to knowing what goes on and why and if they keep it up, they can take the longest lunch and holidays, safe in the knowledge that they are valued and indispensable. But for the majority of office workers, those who are safe in their little cubicles, minimal responsibility is sufficient responsibility. So let them be.

For those who want to get ahead, they have to prove that they're not simply responsible for themselves, but they can be responsible for one other, then another, then five, ten, even fifty thousand other people. Positions of responsibility have leverage over other peoples' responsibility, status, and security. The more people, machines, assets (and who knows what else) you are responsible for, the more you get paid. Simple.

So, people fake, lie, bully and buy their way into positions of responsibility which they subsequently have to defend, while most of us are honest and hard working and strive to get there without a trail of blood behind us. We desperately want it all to be clean and to receive a fair reward that recognises our true and destined status. But no matter how one gets there, what people are paid for and proudly responsible for, is what makes them accountable and therefore liable to get their arses kicked. Responsibility is one thing (you can be proud to be responsible), accountability is another (you fear being accountable), and in any office, where knowledge is the currency and people make decisions, if a fault is found, blame will not be far behind. If the fault, and hence blame, is wrongly apportioned it doesn't matter. It's there because it's part of the game of competition. If you're hit with blame, you lose some of that hard won responsibility.

So, it's no surprise that people in positions of responsibility fake, lie, bully, and buy their way out of being accountable while those of us who are honest but jaded, hard working but exhausted, delegate minions to do our dirty work. All that really counts for being responsible and accountable is to be able prove that you can be trusted with what you've got, and regardless of the moral outcome, show that you can get the job done and simultaneously deal with your competitors.

Status

People need to feel part of something (whether it is a tribe, a team or just a gang of hoodlums) and after a period of initiation in that group, people are given a status (hunter, team psychoanalyst, the guy with the flick-knife). And according to this status we can live out our days with our destiny partially assured, as long as we perform, and gain pride from our status. Until we get bored or we want more.

At this point the hunter in the tribe takes on the chief, the team psychoanalyst masterminds the team leader's plunge into depression, and the guy with the flick-knife ousts the gang's leader.

In a less aggressive way status can be gained rationally and peacefully – people retire, are fired, change jobs, have children, revert to childish nature, or get promoted up and out. There is then a need for someone to take over, and before you know it, you're apparently responsible and now you have a new status. Get ready to feel the force of competition – where previously you were a minion, now you have added responsibility, accountability and status, so people are out to get you. They become competition. They want what you've got. Live it up.

Status feels good, and the pain of responsibility and accountability ebbs with time and privilege, and before you know it, you're wiser, older, and set. This is how you always wanted it. Status is something to be proud of.

Security

Security sits at both ends of the prize – it is a constant. No matter how high or low you're aiming, you want security at the beginning, the middle, and the end.

For the majority of people, security represents a nearby destination, and any point beyond that is deemed too risky. They are happy where they are. Their status is derived from their little secure domain.

For those who seek more lofty positions and take on risk to get there, security comes at a price. It has to be savagely defended or fought for – depending on the position. Detractors will ask: Is the position needed? Is it overpaid? Is it perhaps outdated? Could it be downsized, changed, scrapped, or outsourced somewhere cheaper? But the bigger the risk, the greater the reward.

The higher profile a position, the more likely the player is to attract ridicule (think of a political leader in a country with a free press). This leads to the impression that it is not that secure – but it is. The higher they are, the more secure they are. But how they actually got there is another matter.

Just Give Me the Money

Responsibility, accountability, status, and security are short-lived – they last as long as the job – whereas money is what people really treasure. Used wisely, money lasts longer and is easily converted into something of more value. Enough has been said about money. There are many arguments and books about money: how to make it, share it, eat it, shit it, and recycle it. There's no shortage of people out there ready to take your money and we can all agree there's a sucker born every minute. This doesn't just refer to paying too much; it also refers to not earning enough.

Concentrate on the money you get for your worth and ignore the petty criminals on the streets stealing wallets and the corporate racketeers in boardrooms fleecing the majority. What's mundanely obvious is that the more valuable you are the more you get rewarded, but remember that value equates to perception, as beauty is in the eye of the beholder. Naturally, in the office, people reach a point whereby they wise up and want remuneration for the time they spend there, not something token, but a significant slice from the pie that is baked to reward the office. So life in the office becomes a race to prove, even if the merits are artificial, who is more important and thus entitled to dive their hand into the purse of profits.

The Prize is the turn in a game whereby we can reward ourselves the most while everyone else is still learning the rules.

I work until beer o'clock – Stephen King

A Fat Slice of the Juicy Pie

What's this? The Prize is just a fat slice of the juicy pie? And are you wondering: How can *I* get involved? The answer: Face first, you already are! Yes, look around, you may have no idea of what goes on and why, but don't be fooled, business and opportunity is all about scouting, spying, sharpening knives, closing in, carving up a healthy portion of the pie on the table, and whisking it away. It's proof of a functioning economy. You may be integral to it, but fed, sadly, on stale crumbs.

The pie is not infinite, it's size is set by supply, demand and resources. To some it's a scam when a certain few gobble down the most and not surprisingly there are always cyclic imbalances and social experiments to try to give everyone a fair slice of the pie yet life is, obviously, not just survival of the fittest, but priority to the smartest and fastest. According to Marx, in *Das Capital* (Capital), the central injustice of capitalism is its exploitation and alienation of labour. His great ideas concerning pie crumbs for some and fat bellies for others were the ingredients to a revolutionary *new* pie: communism! But sure enough, in a system that promised equal parts of the pie to all, a few greedy pie eaters clawed their way to the top and caused a mammoth exploitation beyond many modern thinkers' dreams. So, shake visions of equal slices from your hungry eyes and it's back to the office with your hungry tummy.

Getting a fat slice of the pie is about vision, planning, acquiring and utilising knowledge, resources and capital at the right time and taking a fat risk. Think of the entrepreneur who (rather than feverishly digs for gold) buys a hundred picks and shovels to sell to the gold diggers during a gold rush, and think of the qualified consultant's swift manoeuvres in supplying much sought after advice to a desperate company on how to abide by a new piece of organisational legislation. Every day a new discovery is made.

The world *is* change. People rise to the occasion. Industries mushroom as other industries dry up or are outsourced somewhere cheaper. As one pie is eaten, another is being baked. Thus the ingredients and flavours of pies change and the people that foresee change and plot a course to it have the brains to reap the rewards; the rest of the world is forced to pay for their services. What governs these things? There is luck, diligence and intelligence. We are all in it but unable to partake in all *of* it. To some, the pie is the golden egg, and to the rest who are minding their own business, unaware of the changes happening around them or the outcome, it can seem as just a scam (namely because they're not part of it).

So how do you know a pie is in the making? It's quite easy because back to Darwinism, it's all about adaptation. Change is evolution. You can bet that in time new skills are required to service the latest fashion to hit humanity. An easy example is to look at the west; infatuated by new toys yet concerned about polluting the planet to death, hence the growth in Information Technology, and a harder one to predict (but potentially just as profitable) the growth in Environmentalism as an industry. From these two examples, think of all the offshoots and avenues where money can be made. Just remember that if you want to be the first to get on board before the ship comes in, you have to swim out to meet it.

One day your Prize may be to assist in the making of a pie, setting it in the oven and patiently smelling the aromas as it cooks. When the time is right, you pull it out, lay it before you, and knife in hand, eyes bulging from your head, tuck into it. Enjoy the feast.

All I know is I'm not a Marxist - Karl Marx

Enlist Now

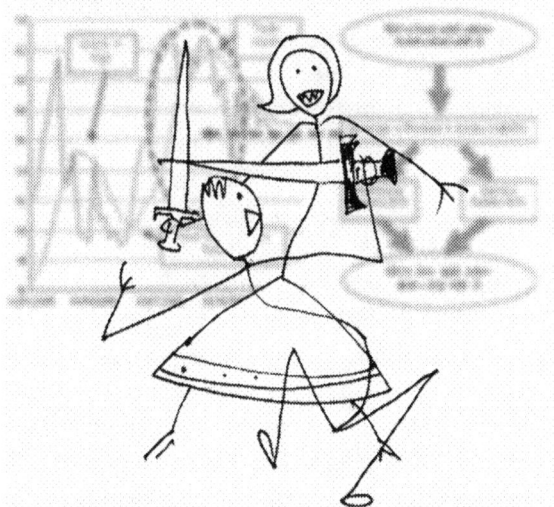

A career, a laugh and a wage...

Time and Place

Just as you made a conscious decision to read *The Art of Office War*, there is an 'affirmative pro-active exuberance' in you to get serious. So let's get one thing straight: Illusions of grandeur will not do. There are many men who would rather have lived as Napoleon; there are many women who think they are Cleopatra. People reach a deluded point sometime in their lives, and decide it is time to do something proactive. They want to get ahead, move up, and understand what goes on. These are admirable thoughts, and thoughts can become action. But the fact is, the majority of people can only move so far within their environment. This is a sobering predicament, which might lead you into thinking that you are a slave to world history or a mere pawn in a corporate shuffle. Yet, because you are in it, no matter how miniscule you actually are, you are riding on the wave of time in one sea that may lead to another ocean. There is an optimistic future out there open to you, but *it is in the future*. You can't read anything concrete about it; we can read history and transplant ourselves back to lavish or worse times, but the future is plain scary and that's where you have to position yourself. Many people are stuck in the past, a few in the present, but the true masters of their own time see into the future. They can afford to be wrong most of the time, but sometimes they will get it right at the right time. And they will prosper.

The future influences the present just as much as the past
– Friedrich Nietzsche

You and the Machine

People choose industries and vice-versa. What you chose, you probably did so based on what was there at the time to burn itself onto your once impressionable little mind. Inevitably you realise what type of cog you are and which way you rotate in the machine. If it wasn't for your acquired industry-specific experience, and hence knowledge, you could fit into any machine, and most probably can.

There is really very little diversity of roles in the office, regardless of the superfluous titles and duties. Therefore there are universal rules and values that can be applied across the board.

If you haven't already, choose an industry based on what excites you for perverse reasons. If you're in an industry, bored or burning out but need to stay put, get excited about changing what you are into something more valuable and become part of the Deal.

The Deal:
Offices & Knowledge Warriors

Knowledge is not about coming up with answers to brain teasers and winning the pub quiz. Knowledge is abstract and all encompassing; you know how to do this, you know about that, you know how to change this and interpret that into something we can use. You work with knowledge and the target or outcome becomes a blinding source of inspiration and reward. It sounds fun and functional, yet it involves tapping endlessly at keyboards, swallowing cold and lumpy feedback, and absorbing what your manager has to enlighten you with. Some complain it's akin to slavery but it doesn't really compare to breaking your whipped-back building a pyramid for a Sun God.

The reason we are slaving away for knowledge is simple: an office job is comfortable; you have to use your brain, and fit into the deal: the larger plan. An office is the brain of an organisation (i.e. a business, a government, a Martian Invasion Force) and is valued for the specific *knowledge* it puts out to the organisation and how the organisation performs in the wider competitive environment.

Without knowledge, an office sinks (so too does its parent organisation), so it is continually sourcing, evaluating and generating knowledge for the benefit of the organisation.

Even though technology has become more sophisticated at gathering information, it is still people that must interpret the data, and carve it out and up into something useful. At this tipping point, knowledge becomes a valuable and a hard-won currency. The organisation recognises that someone needs to prove that they can be trusted with the responsibility and status to use this valuable knowledge for the organisation's gain and thus extract their reward: money, responsibility, status, long lunch, a slice of the pie.

By design and human initiative, organisations have different people working on different aspects of their industry-specific knowledge. The more specific the knowledge and outcome, the safer and easier it is for people to profit from – at the expense of the people in question becoming pigeonholed and tiered to their specific knowledge. The more generic and profitable the knowledge and outcomes, the higher the chance that those involved will proclaim their knowledge as the most valuable, overlapping and colliding with others. Everyone must 'work together' for a common cause and everyone is entitled to a point of view but when there is a difference of opinion there will be a conflict to own the most 'perceived' valuable knowledge because that's what people are rewarded for. Now people play at knowing valuable things they don't to exclaiming that damning knowledge they already knew actually came from someone else. The Knowledge Terrain of Office Conflicts is explained later

Therefore industries rely on knowledge; organisations require their staff to be warriors for knowledge. Millions of people have careers fighting for knowledge and they go to great pains to prove their knowledge ability. It's all about what you know, knowing it better than your competition, and delivering valuable knowledge to the key decision makers.

Stepping back from the numbing enormity of it all, your own field of operations may be safe and secure, so it may be enough to simply recognise your limitations, but it is also important to your job and career to know your competitors' capabilities. Know what they know, perhaps not all of it, but enough. Some people, as we will see, have no hungering to know more than necessary. But if you want to get ahead, learn to like the mundane. Crave knowledge. Brains don't get fat from excess.

Remember: Knowledge is Power, Anytime, Anywhere.

But before you shift into a higher gear, re-acquaint yourself with the people around you.

Even knowledge has to be in the fashion, and where it is not, it is wise to affect ignorance – Baltasar Gracian

Colleagues

Divided We Stand, United We Fall

There are thousands of ways to get to know your colleagues, some fun, and some mundane. Play team sports, get drunk together, group hypnosis, or walk into work late with a sawn-off shotgun and see how fast they run. In reality, very few of us have the real time and patience to get to really know our colleagues, besides having to work with them is taxing enough, so learn to classify people, and fast.

Emotion taints reality. At a basic level people crave harmony, yet they are caught between trusting others too much or too little. By default they aim to please, to not be a hindrance, unless they want something. In this case they will behave however they like to get what they want, depending on what is tolerated. If you meet someone and are already familiar with them through gossip, ignore what you have heard and trust your instinct.

Knowledge also taints reality. Buy ten books on the subjects of human behaviour, leadership traits, sharpening your memory and anything else that provides you with fantasies that are potentially quasi-superior and intimidating. Randomly highlight sections in the books, insert bookmarks, dog-ear pages, and arrange the pile of books on your desk for all to see (it's OK to place *The Art of Office War* on the top of the pile). Watch people slow down and incline their heads as they read the titles on the spines, and then race away in a hurry. People are scared of analytical evaluation because it might reveal their weaker points. You don't even have to read the books; all you have to do is bluff with knowledge. Watch how people have been doing the same to you.

Money is an indicator. Remember that everyone is selected to work in an office for a reason, someone pays them for doing something. Even in the civil service (government) where the majority of people do very little, they nonetheless achieve something: They create valid reasons why taxes should be used to pay them – that's their duty, that's what they do extremely well, but they'll never earn too much no matter how much they protest and strike . Similarly, in the mightiest and meanest of cost-cutting corporations that are bent on siphoning a profit 24/7 out of every tangible asset available in their globalised world until it all crashes in a depression, there will be people coasting along in one of the several layers of tolerate, institutional bureaucracy. They've found a safe place to exist and they probably get paid well. All around the world people are getting paid because they've proven their value to the market (which is driven by society's needs), but in many cases they shouldn't be paid or even paid less. Too much analysis of it all will give you a headache.

On a grander scale, something that may one day be noted in the chunky history books and regarded as a pinnacle of fatty success or survival finesse over our environment, is the Western Age of Excess. Thanks to geopolitics, the free-market, social and technological revolutions and an inherent sense of order from an obedient citizenship (plus a thousand other things), we can feed and pay ourselves extremely well, enjoy a luxury lifestyle, and still complain ad nauseam. The West is so wealthy that there is an abundance of jobs that keep people in the knowledge and services industry, doing God knows what. This is the flipside of advanced civilisation – there are people who are paid and happy to work, yet don't contribute a great amount to the world. They even find it hard to measure their worth and hence alleviate their absence of purpose by performing niche tasks that enable them to reign supreme, such as stamp collecting, sports, and other chic perversions. But they will be productive when they are called upon to assist the hard working people who make things happen. The latter lead the way and build stuff (like bridges, trade agreements, space-rockets), correct the world's mistakes, maintain the civilisation we enjoy so much, and ignite revolutions.

Universal Hard Worker. Hard workers are hard workers because they have valid incentives; which go beyond the lust for security, responsibility and status, and a fat ego. Think of the satisfaction of completing something, the pleasure of having an occupied mind, and money. Amusingly, they are not hard workers because of some romantic notion of a work ethic, for it must be noted that they are usually paid more than their lazier comrades. This does not mean justice follows hard work. People being people, there are low paid, lazy people jealous of highly paid, hard workers, and there are also low paid, hard workers jealous of lazy, highly paid leaches. There is incredible injustice in the office, whereas in the jungle, it's plain life and death.

Find out what your colleagues are up to. What do they want? What do you want? Just to stay in your position and do what you were hired for? Advancement depends upon the acquisition of new skills and taking on extra tasks. But by snatching extra tasks from those around you who are lazy, you are stealing their reasons for employment. Take more. Take less. It is up to you. In any position, in any organisation, you must know everything about your position and every other position. To move up you must train someone with all the skills you know and bequeath them your responsibility so that they can step into your shoes and you can move up, or sideways and then up. Some people adopt dirty tricks to advance themselves – do not observe them and them only. Observe everyone around you and what is tolerated. Know why and how they conform to the system when the system should be spitting them out.

Understanding colleagues isn't that hard. In this chapter you will learn the equivalent of three university years, but sadly without the wild parties, sex, silly drugs, adventures in rock'n'roll/techno, bad hangovers and student debt.

Permanents vs. Temps

Permanent and temporary (including contingent and contractors) staff exist in a strange paradox. Each envies the benefits of the other, but given the chance to swap they would choose to remain in their respective slots. It's a case of security vs. time: a sacrifice of one or the other depending on the side of the fence you work on.

Permanents seem to have a better deal: they are harder to dismiss, can receive holiday, sick and severance pay and bonuses, and promotions, but they have to abide by employers' conditions.

Conditions equals restrictions causing resentment so permanents are likely to work the system; temporary staff are paid by the hour to do the work the permanents have learnt to tactfully and lazily avoid. Temporary staff are the safest option for all the demanding and/or shit jobs; temps are easy to hire (except for the expensive and their expertise), are malleable to tasks, and if they aren't of any use, dismissible in a matter of minutes, proof that slavery is far from extinct, it has simply evolved into a lucrative business re-branded as 'recruitment'. In the office recognise that permanents are probably there for the long run, until retirement with all its benefits, whereas temps are there for the day, and if they tow the line, they may work tomorrow. However, permanent staff, though smugly enjoying their job security (thanks to new laws they're not so dismissible as in yesteryear, hence it's safer to hire disposable temps), are restricted to a fixed amount of holiday time per year based on their status. In retaliation, some permanents treat their job as a second holiday; tasks can be stretched out to fill the time available until some higher authority kicks them in the shins. Permanents have the time and mental space to play political in the workplace for the long run, until of course, the higher authority instigates a purging of the dead wood. Now call in the temps to carry the load.

Temporary staff are valued because their motivation, obvious by their decision not to become permanent, is not to ensconce themselves in the office, and are unlikely to devise some devious plan to acquire an abundance of un-due responsibility, power and knowledge wealth, leading to a plain-sailing lazy career. It seems temporary staff are there for the quick money and not much else. They gain experience and may become permanent, but they can only do so after they have proved their worth. But most importantly, temporary staff command their work (they can just as easily leave as they arrived: it's their choice) and holiday time; time not working with people like you, not money, is their precious commodity.

Active vs. Passive, Boring vs. Extreme, and the Herd

As far as psychology goes, there are many classifications concocted by witty industry professionals to confuse us, but it's better to keep it simple. When it comes to work ethics, people can be categorised as either active or passive.

Active People are hard working; they work for personal, family, financial or other motivations.

Passive People perform in order to have for the basic necessities; they strive to live the most and contribute the least. They want minimal responsibility and are usually rewarded with the minimum wage.

Emotionally there are two types of people, **The Boring** and **The Extreme**.

The Boring only appear boring when they are compared to the Extreme, but for the sake of typecasting, the Boring will not rock the boat, raise undue objections, or 'excite' people into 'rebellious' activities. If there is a gene therapy for the Boring, it probably wouldn't help, because some people just prefer to be plain *boring*.

The Extreme people have something to do or say, for better or for worse, and fill the void created by the Boring. The more entertaining an Extreme person is, the more threatening they are to the civilised *status quo* of any office. Quite often the Extreme people, who are vastly outnumbered by the Boring, are not fired or retrenched, because like indoor plants, they provide a sense of life. And they're usually the people that get things done.

The mix of **Active** and **Passive**, **Boring** and **Extreme** plays an important part in any office because too much of one breed leads to an imbalance, and people of different sets are always in conflict. Learn to pigeonhole people rather than trying to understand the complexities of their character, because like it or not they've probably already labelled you.

Active and Passive, Boring and Extreme is a very simple means of understanding your colleagues as individuals, so here are some additional markers of human behaviour which relate to the **Herd**:

The Leaders. The alpha male/female, those born to win, the captains of industry, the movers and shakers. With leaders it is important to grasp what they have to grasp; are they just a dispensable manager of a herd of easily-downsizeable drones in a global company, or is their business *really* their business – so if it goes down, so does their house, family, and the pet dog may go hungry.

The former type, those leaders who are safely embedded in an organisation that is not their own, are more susceptible to the fusing of their power and ego into a sycophantic and paranoid mess. And yet they maintain a veneer of dictatorial responsibility and bullet-proof status. They lose their rational faculties as their master, the organisation, grooms them into becoming the perfect product of the organisation. It must be noted that the personality traits of these leaders trickles down to the people below them, so that some of the minions emulate the leader as he/she/it emulates the organisation. These leaders are also artful at avoiding accountability for the fuss they cause – they can shift blame like a magician pulling a fluffy white rabbit out of a dusty black hat.

The Followers. People enjoy following a good leader; it is in our genes. But it can easily be confused with being a yes-man, one of the lambs, the intolerable sloth, or the meek and weak. There is nothing wrong with following, unless it's a lemming over a cliff.

The Audience. Think of all the complainers, agitators, and whingers who complain, 'you should have done it this way', and yet they never risk anything themselves. And still they applaud at appropriate moments, or else they get fired.

Intellectual Terrorists. There's one in every bunch. They are not leaders, or complainers, they represent a lone voice of reason in a sea of subservience. According to corporate propaganda 'creative input' is highly valued, but only if it comes from consultants and those up the ladder who are paid more for their supposedly 'enlightened' and 'educated' perspective on how to run things they aren't involved with. If 'creative input' comes from other quarters, then the person is labelled a loner, an agitator, or worse still, Intellectual Terrorist. Watch out.

People are people; it is good to know what they're on about superficially, but to know too much will only make you sorry for them. Don't take the bait. Don't try to change them. Know what you are to them, and they to you.

Friends

Friends are usually not in competition with you, but if they are know that they see more to life than inter-competition in the office. Friendship is dialogue, philosophy, humour and sadness, not to be wasted with idiots.

In the workplace there are several types of friends: those you entertain and in who entertain you through personal anecdotes, sex life, substance abuse, narcissistic traits. Then there are friends that are 'neutral'; your range of conversation topics is safe, because you don't truly click with them, and as humans are social critters, we feel compelled to chat. All types of friends can betray you except one: the friend that is on par with your emotional stance towards the office. The emotional bond you consequently have with them creates an alliance, and providing competition doesn't intervene, you can trust them. This is the type of valuable friend who stabs you in the front, not the back.

Friendship multiplies the good of life and divides the evil
- Baltasar Gracian

Enemies

Enemies are enemies, pure and simple. Instead of projecting goodwill to them, trying to convince you and them that their nasty persona is simply a product of institutional mistreatment, stunted emotional maturity, jealousy, or anything else easily explainable that makes their behaviour forgivable, just think of them as possessed by evil spirits. They will steal your milk, spread gossip, poison or steal your ideas, and smile civilly before they strike. Smile back, not with rosy warmth, but black ice.

Enemies are out to get you. Sometimes there are a plethora of un-decipherable reasons forming their twisted logic as to why they are your enemy, but mostly probably they see you as a threat. If it's obvious why they see you as a threat (ie, competing for the same promotion?) then their methods will be very cunning. Watch your back. Soon you will know what to look out for.

But if you can't understand why someone is an enemy yet they see you as a threat, don't sit and analyse the situation and conjure up methods to diffuse something you can't grapple with, hoping to turn their mind around, because they will continue their mode of operations anyway – to remove or injure you the threat. And there you are wasting precious energy and your time by hoping you can make peace and spread harmony while they are plotting your downfall! If someone is your enemy, draw them close, watch them, and never forget their intent.

> *Keep your friends close, and your enemies closer*
> *– Roman proverb*

Rivalries

Rivalries involve competition, and healthy friendships, but what is not said is as dangerous as what is. Rivalries will encourage the stealing of ideas and the spread of gossip. Rivals appear to help you when you need no help. Rivals may be more noble than enemies but they cannot be trusted.

- Enemies are spoiled minds and are enemies forever.
- Rivals will offer the lure of friendship while isolating you.
- Beware the rival that appears too friendly.

The benefit of rivals is that you can work with them on a mutually-beneficial project with a clearly understood objective. Two heads are better than one, but keep the cards on the table and straight down the line. The best aspect of a rival is that you can exchange valuable information, furthermore you learn more about yourself when you have something to rival.

Iron sharpens Iron – Roman proverb

80% Passive Cannon Fodder

Apparently 20% of people get things done, 80% don't and if they do, it's all in their own time. They are the masses, generally passive and boring, and usually set in their ways. These people provide a social marker, a benchmark of what not to be if you really want to get somewhere. Obviously this is all in the eye of the beholder, but when do we ever all see eye-to-eye? There has to be disparity in the world, so there have to be Cannon Fodder and Ambitious Fuckers. The world needs followers, drones, and cannon fodder otherwise we wouldn't have anyone weak to pick on when we crave a simple ego boost derived from someone else's neurological misfortune. The meek may inherit the earth, and you with them, but until then use them as a buffer, a cushion and a net. They are the ones who massage your ego and inspire, they will spy for you, but probably think you're a waste of space too.

While they might seem harmless or docile in the office, they might well be wild and crazy in their own time. Most people see work as a means of living peacefully – they don't want to be involved in power struggles, hyper-sensitive gossip, mind-altering revolutionary ideas, and above all, change. Change for them is as dangerous as wearing the same socks twice in a week. For them using the system as it uses them, coupled with the weary notion of 'working for the man', is all part of life. They could be coerced into believing that the universe isn't expanding outwards, it is accelerating inwards, or that the world is flat and getting flatter, but they would stick to one basic tenet – I have a job and I'm not going to lose it.

With respect to power play, they have one simple rule that governs their behaviour – the need for security. Because they are not going to rise to a position of power, they will ally themselves with a main power source and sit there, fat and happy. Don't be disgusted with their lack of lustre for life; praise them because they are hardly a threat. Utilise their lack of spark at work by getting them to spy for you on some aspect of office rivalry, so that it becomes a shared entertainment.

Society has always seemed to demand a little more from human beings than it will get in practice – George Orwell

Ambitious Fuckers

What drives ambition? What ignites the engine of success? What inspires greatness? If you're not on this train to riches, do you give a fuck? Even if you are one yourself, you can't ignore Ambitious Fuckers. On the one hand they are ambitious, on the other they'll fuck you over before sunrise, and you'll only catch the imprint of their fist in your face at the very end of the day.

Much of Ambition cannot be taught. Purchasers of MBAs will tattoo those three little letters on their foreheads and proclaim themselves Masters of Business of the Universe but true masters of business don't need an MBA – they are the business. They eat business for breakfast and really have no choice in the matter, they are programmed that way. Ambition is an elusive characteristic that creates a powerful person, and if you have to work with (or against) an Ambitious Fucker, observe them. On the one hand you will learn valuable things; on the other you will see their weaknesses and their dark side. You will come to understand what really drives them and why you won't drive with them *all the way*.

Ambitious Fuckers are the deal-hungry salesman, the hot-shot marketing genius, the icy PR queen who knows all the celebrities, and the top gun corporate hero who was promoted from pimple-faced mail boy to CEO in only seven cat years. Other dangerous Ambitious Fuckers are those that have risen, and will never rise again, but they will fight tooth and nail to hold on to their position. They have attained their little 'high ground', and their ambition is to stay there until they retire, or someone fires them. If they see you rising above your station for half a second they'll liquidate your responsibilities to bring you down to a more manageable size.

Ambition thrives in a power vacuum. If you removed the ambitious manager from a team that operated in a fast paced and rewarding environment, and promoted a passive player to their position, there is a good chance the passive would turn into the active, rise to the captaincy, and unleash their inner ambition.

Throughout history many people have emerged from obscurity to a station of greatness, yet in life many who seek greatness have faded straight into obscurity. Was all the ambition worth it? Yes, for some people ambition, success or failure is their life.

If you need to navigate around an Ambitious Fucker here are a few tips:

- ✦ Stay out of their way unless you can face their fury.
- ✦ Don't try to be their confidante. Let conniving fools play at that. Be completely honest with the Ambitious and they'll come to you.
- ✦ Don't waste their time.
- ✦ If you need their help, ask them. The best way to get something done is to ask a busy person.

Ambition is like love, impatient both of delays and rivals
– Buddha

The Boss

The boss is the established knowledge chief, the line, middle, lower (or whatever) manager, the team leader, the overseer, the enlightened one, or perhaps simply the lucky idiot who was in the right place at the right time for an undeserved promotion. The boss and management in general, are not to be feared because they must also answer to *their* boss, shareholders and investors.

Your immediate boss is not the fearsome being that your foolish colleagues hold in esteemed awe. Your boss throws tantrums, barks orders or turns on the charm to get what they want, even though they know they're nothing, easily replaceable, and any one of you could do their job. The more childish and vicious a boss, the more likely the role isn't that hard.

All that a boss does is what you do, but at a higher level. They are the one in the position of power to manage lots of people like you, take all the knowledge you create, and mix it into something that can be nailed to the wall to impress *their* boss.

However, if you don't like your boss and wish to initiate change, shift the paradigm and all that, sadly for you, the buck stops with them. If you don't like them, move on.

The Owner

The owner possesses some of the qualities of a leader as well as a boss. They are the ones that do what most people wouldn't dare to do and that is why they work for them. How many people would actually leave their safe little job and start their own business, where they manage, hire, fire and train people to operate their business? Knowing full well that if it were to fail, everyone but the owner could easily walk away? On the other hand, if it were to succeed, the owner is the one who reaps the reward and takes on a growing responsibility. Owners of businesses that have an office are tight-arses, not because they like to be, but because that one dollar of liquid paper you stole last week means one dollar less for paying off debts, banks, your wages, and their profits.

The Veterans

Veterans should not be given a rank, because there is no justice as to why the wise are at the bottom and the fools at the top. That's just one of the many ways the system organises itself: "We need young blood at the helm, and all the veterans, pushing from the rear".

Some veterans are at the top and set in their ways, and some aren't. Some see farther than any new kid on the block. As with war veterans, there is no sure-fire solution as to what to do with them. Sometimes they are worked to their grave, pigeonholed for their antique views and methods, their loyalty is taken for granted, they are kept around like a monument to the 'glory years', or treated like part of the furniture. Regardless of how they are treated, they are good for one thing: knowledge. If you encounter a problem, talk to a veteran (or coax them into talking talk to you – bribe them with something symbolic, like a nice cup of tea or coffee and a sweet pastry), and you will find that there really is nothing new under the sun. You will even find out things erased from the official office history, and once you have the *good* gossip, you have a weapon.

The View from the Top

The last and most decisive divider between staff is based on caste, class and accelerated personal development – some are at the very top, and everyone else is not. The latter are the plebeians, a lovely term from 'romantic' times, used to describe the common people of Rome. The former are the alphas, 'alpha' being the first letter of the Greek alphabet, and a term synonymous with 'greater than the rest'.

For Plebs there is more to life than the mundane world of work and toil, there is a life out of work hours and that's reason they work – to enjoy life. Their working attention span goes from 9am to 5pm. Unlike their counterparts in ancient Rome, moderns Plebs have choices, education (at a hefty price) and mobility; in the office they can move between professions and industries. These shifts may brighten their careers, but it is still the notion of a comfortable and hopefully satisfying life that makes them happy. Believe it or not, many people have no desire to be super successful, but they may work hard and play the system if they wish, and with a bit of luck and a lot of connections develop and elevate themselves to the position of Alpha.

Once you wipe away an Alpha's veneer, you will find that they are not super successful. Alphas rule the world from privileged positions; they are at the top of the pyramid and abide by the 'corporate management' that controls the Plebs. Alphas use to be found amongst chiefdoms and royalty, but as revolutions spread, and globalised trade mushroomed, merchants and then the educated (MBAs) became the new breed of Alphas. They climbed the ranks of corporations and lifted each other higher and higher, until they all sat on the board of directors. These Alphas manage companies they don't own, they set their own remuneration regardless of success or failure, they create or axe jobs, and are safe from plebeian angst and revolution by the laws of the land – which they can easily misconstrue in their own favour. Though there have been some spectacular Alpha falls, there are a great many out there who continue to 'defraud the system' as the majority of disgruntled Plebs interpret it, or just 'serve the market', as the many observant Alphas study it.

In every state, be it capitalist, market economy, social democratic, communist or despotic, there are the Alphas and the Plebs: the have-mores and having-less-and-lessers. Disparity between the two is a constant; each thinks the other has no idea what they're doing. In this current period of globalisation (which is not a new phenomenon) and speedier communication, change is rapid: people and entities can alter mindsets and technology to meet demand. So if a company, like a state, is doing fine and all are happily remunerated and subdued by propaganda, what's the use in creating an uprising or revolution? Particularly when the majority have no desire for change? There will always be a quiet understanding and thus harmony between the Plebs and the Alphas until change from the outside environment affects the inside environment. And yet even though everything seems peaceful, beneath the calm surface is a murky undertow where The Art of Office War rages. This is the control, threat, execution, and/or bluffing of knowledge.

Competition & Conflict

Jack and Jill were real team players...

Lock and Load

Competition and conflict are like two hands washing each other, yet competition is regarded as healthy whereas conflict is not. Competition inevitably leads to conflict. Anyone who says your methods of getting what you want 'lead to conflict, so they are savage, unhealthy and counter-productive' is probably trying to veil the true nature of their invasive and stealthy attack on you to keep you out of the competition. They are misleading you, so that you drown in a swamp of guilt.

Thanks to the violent history our civilisation rests on, we wish to be at peace and hope friction in our life just simmers away, evaporating into a fluffy cloud of peace. The days of skull smashing tribal feuds, aristocratic pistol duelling and good old arm wrestling are over, because the pen is sharper than the sword, and a lot healthier. But conflict is a constant, and in the office it emerges as subversive conflict. On the one hand we want to run into the car park and swing our fists, but on the other we're trying to be civil and being civil means getting what we want in other ways, though they might not be pacifist.

Though first impressions may scare you, people really do mean well. They are working for the supreme cause: keep the boss happy and the organisation earning money. Although these two fundamentals unite staff, they also create the greatest of competition: what if someone considers their knowledge superior, and concludes they have the best ideas, so they garner favour from a manager, deliberately making your ideas appear worthless? What happens when friendly competition turns into open conflict? Beat the war drum, have a little a war dance, pray to your ancestors for safety in battle, and load your brain full of information to counteract your foe. Knowledge is the key to a chest full of fabulous riches and everyone wants to own it.

Remember that everyone has a secret weapon, an ace up their sleeve, a reason to think they're invincible. But they also have an

Achilles heel, and most importantly a grudge to bear. Rivals will fight tooth and nail over shared yet scarce resources; cannon fodder will thwart ambitious fuckers by withholding information. Enemies sew the seed of conflict in the most benign of ways and watch with pleasure as weeds grow between the best of friends (not because they have some sort of strategy – they do it because they *can*). On the outside all staff are your friends, so beware when civility extends too far – an office glimmering with icy smiles is rich with warmly stabbed backs.

Because from one day to the next you do not know what form conflict will take and how it may damage you, you must live day to day knowing that shit can hit the fan at any moment. For the discipline of science this unpredictability is called entropy. This does not entail walking down the office hallway with an erect back, notebook and pen ready to note any malicious detail; it means that every day you must be aware of your position in relation to each of your required tasks. Your best defence is to observe and be aware. This arms you with the greatest weapon and tactic you could ever wish for – flexibility. Your instinct senses conflict, and gives you time to decide whether to be defensive or on the offensive. You might also simply want to observe someone else's conflict unfolding like a set-piece naval battle of titanic proportions. When people know you are aware, they will not implicate you in petty conflicts.

Before all else, be armed – Niccolo Machiavelli

Causes of Conflict

There is always a cause that precedes conflict, and when opposing parties are hot under the collar and creating a scene, the cause is called upon to diffuse the situation. Nonetheless, because conflict is about competition, the competitors have a strategy in mind, so in the heat of battle or the frantic rush through a peace signing process, they will try to erase or distort the roots of the conflict and alter the situation towards a favourable outcome. Often the claimed cause is a red-herring, so the real cause is left to be fought over again after both feuding parties have licked their wounds.

The following are some prime causes of conflict:

Misunderstanding + Ego + Competition = Conflict

A subtle 'misunderstanding' is often seen as a common source of workplace strife, but when someone wants to be proved right and there are multiple egos involved, while the opposing parties might civilly say there is a 'misunderstanding', the truth is simple: conflict must decide the competition. This is common enough and before you know it, the passive crawl out of their shells and become active, there is a reward (sometimes miniscule) plus the desired outcome is the protection of one's domain, and even you may feel the need to assert yourself in ways never tried before. Before you lock horns, work out exactly who you are dealing with, and probe their attack. If someone wants to get their way then the misunderstanding will probably relate to your weak subject area, because they are strong and they want to win. Don't think that there really has been a *misunderstanding*. Just take a big breath. Let them fire the first shot to ascertain where they're aiming and how they're going to get the world to believe they're right. You need to know their tactics in order to turn it back on them.

Fact vs Fiction

What was a fact yesterday is fiction today, and tomorrow's fiction is today's fact. There is a myriad of ways to create fact out of fiction, and vice versa. Many people will change what is fact and fiction on a daily basis, not to dazzle you, or to confuse or outwit you with new and interesting knowledge, but because their information environment is in permanent flux and they believe it is right to ride it. Conflicts arise at climatic points, when two or more people come up with different points of view from roughly the same information, or they arrive at the same point of view but need to establish who got there first. Each is fighting from the high ground for the high ground. They'll scream the facts down your throat, and a little part of you will want to clutch at a belief. But in times of conflict, you must decipher what is fact and fiction and choose neither. Nothing should sway your mind until you have really heard all the details.

There are no eternal facts, as there are no absolute truths
– Friedrich Nietzsche

Factions vs. Individualism

A faction's information resource is confined, and defined by, what they know best. They are open to ideas from trusted sources (including the faction's collective imagination), and occasionally fluctuate from within the faction's conservative borders. The faction is comfortable with a slight flux of information, it is alive and unified, and will greet an individual's offer of different and conflicting information in two ways:

1. The faction's unity relies on defending itself from other factions' information as well as information from crazed individuals. Any individualism will be initially dismissed as intellectual terrorism.

2. Once an individual decides to confront a faction, the faction's collective strength will dutifully dissect the negative points of an individual's information.

Individualism will not sway a faction until the faction swallows the ideas from within itself and makes them their own, and performs a subtle re-branding.

To avoid conflict, and to ease the process of the absorption of an individual's idea into a faction's manifesto, it has to be planted politically, poetically but also rationally, with the assistance of quite fictitious arguments. Think of high paid consultants.

Many individuals think that sheer righteousness, the triumph of good over evil, and other such fairytale nonsense will move mountains. Not so. As most factions are composed of passive cannon-fodder nodding to what the ambitious fuckers say, the individual must recognise that they themselves pose a threat and until they get inside the competition, they will remain an enemy on the outside.

There is nothing more difficult to take in hand, more perilous to conduct, or more uncertain in its success, than to take the lead in the introduction of a new order of things – Niccolo Machiavelli

Friendly Competition

The end result of friendly competition is not to disrupt friendship but to decide a competition. If at the end of the competition (regardless of the outcome) the friendship is spoilt, so what? If a competition is spoilt through friendship, so what? Both come and go. But a friendly competition does accelerate the end result of both – will the friendship last, and who will win the competition? There is nothing to be afraid of in a friendly competition – iron sharpens iron and you will learn more about yourself than just playing it passive and cool with your friend.

Head Stomping – Removing You from the Competition

While it is pleasing to the mind to think of all humans as benevolent creatures, never underestimate the ability of people to stomp on your head. They do this because:

- ⊕ They don't like you.
- ⊕ They see you as a threat.
- ⊕ They stomp on heads to feed their ego.

In the wild, it is normal for siblings to eat each other in the nest in times of hunger so don't get emotional when a work colleague comes down hard on you. Think of it as a blessing – at least you are not a harmless boring passive.

Worker Bee vs. Queen Bee

The worker sees the world at a different level to the queen. The worker feels they know the terrain in their sector, while the queen feels she knows the entire field of operations. Both will be right, but when a decision is made that troubles one of them, how long they remain troubled is a sign of how flexible they are.

If we could all see the other side we would live in harmony, walk naked like Adam, Eve and the annoying hippies, but we are human and we are flawed because of greedy needs and bright ideas. So if you work for the queen bee and you're just a worker bee, sometimes you must grin and bear it, or buzz off to another hive. If you stay, be prepared to listen and obey the queen bee. Most people in high positions, regardless of how they got there and remain there, usually know something you don't. They are paid to listen to you and a thousand other buzzing bees like you every day. Besides, at the end of the day someone has to take charge and assume responsibility.

In the beginner's mind there are many possibilities,
in the expert's mind there are few – Shunryu Suzuki

Politics

Is the feeling of doomed harmony within a political faction worth the fight to defend the ideals? Is there a place for politics in the office when allegiances to personalities and ethical ideals are over-shadowed by the basic need for a weekly wage?

If you are unflinchingly political, that is your strength, and people will trust, like, detest and most of all respect you because you hold your ground and constitute an easy target. Competitors may feel cheap if they attacked you on the obvious political points, so a vested interest can serve as a defence. It can also act as a magnet – a challenge for your enemies to pick you to bits for your convictions.

But if you merely dabble in politics, mainly for the spice of an argument to punctuate your day, you may be easily coerced into positions that are definitely not you.

It is comforting to belong to something, admirable even, but with a force of mind comes a minefield of dangers. Sometimes politics is used as the excuse for conflict, and when it is politics that is the centre of the dispute, the conflict will be played out over a 'side issue'. In the boredom of the office, politics may be fickle, but it can also be fun.

In politics, stupidity is not a handicap – Napoleon Bonaparte

Envy and Jealousy

Conformity in the office is everywhere, think of partitioned cubicles equal in size relative to rank, the careful measuring of units and labour, conduct, processes and ceremony, 'shirt and tie' or 'neat casual' uniform dress codes. These things seem to iron out our frailest emotions. How can anything be un-equal when we're treated all the same?   But the system that was created and streamlined by humans for humans to perform their little tasks and little else, falls victim to those who are programmed to be envious and jealous. Like washed-up coconuts on a desert island, envy and jealousy can root and grow.

Envy and jealousy, though seemingly effaced by office ergonomics, are the main drivers and motivation of people. You want that new car that Jenny in accounting bought last month? Well you work hard. You covert Bill's position – well you undermine him, get him pigeon-holed and sent to re-training so you can take over.

Conflict Decides and Entertains

Conflict also erupts because something has to be decided, someone has to be on top, someone has to know their place. Furthermore people like the entertaining spectacle and will sit back, watch conflict prepare itself and applaud it into the arena, cheer the fight and even weep as the defeated (or what is left of them) is carted off. If there are no apparent reasons for conflict, if something simply shatters the sterile fragility of the friendly office facade, do not be alarmed. Things erupt from the slightest provocation because we are social creatures; we crave drama and if an office is in a state of peace, start something. Push a few buttons. Arouse some extreme people into action. Create a little conflict and see if you can control it, after all you only live once. You may unwittingly be creating conflicts, you may fancy yourself as a great mediator, and you may like to unleash your sharp tongue. What would life be like without proving your true traits?

Give the people bread and circuses – Roman Proverb.

Facing Conflict

When conflict comes, don't feel ashamed at the impulse to run. The animal instinct to run from terror has kept us alive and ahead of rising biblical floods, apocalyptic lava flows and the hungry sabre tooth tiger. But we are in the future now, so you can't just run. Besides you're in an office, so where are you going to run to? We all have our escape methods (calling in sick, and avoiding the issues) but sooner or later you have to deal with it – and sooner rather than later is preferable. These things just don't go away and fortunately the first civil step in any office to tackle the big issue of conflict is to sing and dance to the archetypal conflict management routine.

The Conflict Management Routine

The doctrine is that we are a united team, one big 'corporate managed' family entwined with a connected global village. Synthetic harmony descends like a medieval plague – some people catch the fever, keel over and surrender to a death of placidity and defeat. The rest hole themselves up in isolation and calculate their next move. There is no family and certainly no village. We are all on our own.

But the appearance of cohesiveness rules the day. After a misunderstanding (codeword for conflict), over-exerted politeness is called upon to cease and smother conflict, so that the disgruntled parties can take the orchestrated steps to resolution. These include gestures such as formulating a specific complaint, resisting the temptation to involve others in the conflict, trying to depersonalise conflicts (the banal "us versus the problem" rather than "me versus you, you fucking idiot" tactic), and finally trying to "listen" very intently to the other's problems before explaining one's own position. The demands of ceremonial niceness go on and on. Don't *always* involve superiors in conflict resolution. If an extended discussion is necessary, agree first on a time and place to 'talk' and perhaps take the issue 'outside' and negotiate away from the office gossip mongers. Limit complaints to abstract terminology. Direct discriminating character assassination is a nasty no-no. Know when conflict isn't just conflict, but when it is actually sexual, racial or ethnic harassment. Consider using a mediator if the issue is too emotional to resolve in a mutual discussion. Involve a supervisor. Don't involve a supervisor. Consider hiring a professional ~~assassin~~ counsellor. Admit your fault first, and wait for theirs. Cover it up in layers of bureaucratic jargon and hope it goes away. Or quit your job citing 'personal differences' – not only does it look good on a CV, it's great trying to explain it to people who depend on your wage, like your family, partners, and the loan shark.

True Conflict

True conflict is how you take conflict your way. Bring your competitor into your trap. Bait them with all the measures that conflict management demands and turn the tables: get personal, bully, misconstrue what they say again and again until they (like everyone else) can't believe/won't know what's going on. Conflict is not to be managed; it is there to be won. Anyone utilising conflict management measures is crushing you with niceties, and simultaneously hacking an axe into your spine. Of course, people must pander to the rituals of conflict management; it is a public code of conduct, but two people in the heat of conflict need to sort out where they stand. Some people are better equipped to drag a conflict out over months, years, even decades. If they see that their competitor likes things sorted out in minutes, they'll trap them into acting with no regard for civility and then dishonour them publicly for as *long* as possible. While true conflict may make you more enemies better equipped to deal with you, inversely people will respect you. Passive people can spend their careers cooking up a conflict but never experiencing the glee of victory or the nausea of defeat that active people do. You might win, you might you lose. And remember, the nasty tactics you use will be used against you.

Re-assure yourself that there is nothing to be afraid of (except offending those who can fire you!), because conflict is an energy that can be harnessed. It is as dangerous as it is healthy, and without competition and conflict we remain in a steady state, whereby nothing changes or adapts to a world that is constantly changing. If you want to bring about change you will have to become a walking conflict.

The prizes of competition are easy to see, but the actual instruments and positions of people that decide conflict are harder to define. How do people get what they want? Fortunately, in the confines of the office, it all translates back to knowledge.

There are no absolute rules of conduct, either in peace or war.
Everything depends on circumstances – Leon Trotsky

The Knowledge
Terrain of Office
Conflict

Knowledge Terrain

True knowledge, worldly experience and higher intelligence, is never sufficiently remunerated, but what we are paid to know – our own expertise and prime reason for employment – has to be defended, rewarded, capitalised upon and armed like a battleship in order to show those responsible for our wages or business that we are worthy of it, and also that they are worthy of us providing it for them. There's always someone who can take your place, so the knowledge you're paid for becomes the legs on which you stand, and can easily be kicked from under you. When the shit hits the fan people normally ask:

- ✦ Who knew it would happen? (responsibility)
- ✦ Who could have acted on it? (accountability)
- ✦ Who knew but didn't act? (responsibility + accountability)
- ✦ Why didn't they act? (knowledge war has begun – who knows best)
- ✦ It was you! (time to defend yourself)
- ✦ OK, so who then? (blame someone else)

When people are delegated duties to do with knowledge, they have to attack, defend, reinforce and constantly evaluate where they are on the knowledge terrain in the office regardless of what they really know.

> *He will conquer who has learnt the art of artifice of deviation.*
> *Such is the art of manoeuvring – Sun Tzu*

Know your terrain by gauging your level of actual and perceived knowledge superiority in a particular domain. And more importantly, determine how others judge your level of knowledge in that domain. Reality is just as important as illusion. Be aware of what you are expected to know in terms of your duty, and likewise for your opponents. Know what you want and what you don't know. Some people may know what you want, others will not, and yet others will have contradictory ideas you couldn't even dream of.

Conflict usually arrives as an invitation initially: add your ideas to this, help so-and-so with that, make changes where required. You are being invited to step into another's domain. If you're not invited, they may already have a piece of your information to pick apart and confront you with later. They will wait until one of their colleagues has baited you and distracted your fresh mind with some petty task. Then they will use the element of surprise and attack. Because knowledge, and the varying shapes it takes, is the key to power in the office you must decide as part of your strategy where you are on the knowledge terrain, and how to manoeuvre on it. Knowledge is not confined. Use knowledge as an enticer for more knowledge; entice people away from what may harm you. It is the art of spin, integrity and resourcefulness, and is as slippery to master as a bowl of spaghetti. You need a fork and spoon to manage it all. These tools are you and how you handle information. Do not waste your energy on futile attacks. Avoid traps. Do not offer a front for your enemy to attack. Although this may sound very abstract and hard to implement, it is what you have to be so you can avoid an attack but in turn attack.

Example:

Knowledge	Jack	Jill
Formal Education	No	Yes
Industry Experience	Yes	No
Product Knowledge	Yes	Yes
Marketing Experience	Yes	No
How to Win Over Management	No	Yes

From the table above it's easy to see where Jack and Jill stand on the knowledge terrain. Jack has a practical edge and Jill has theoretical and diplomatic superiority. For Jill to try and use her knowledge of industry and marketing knowledge is futile because she has little compared to Jack, but she may get her way because she's educated and knows how to win over management, something Jack has no idea about.

Low Ground – Knowledge Poor

Fate and duty has it that you are in the low ground. You know little or nothing. Anyone can attack you. If you wish to move from the low ground into a particular area, study and make an ally in that area. If you have to defend the low ground, use any tactic which evades conflict in the low ground – after all, you know nothing or not enough to be accountable for it. If someone is out to squash you, and they can, they will. Move the nature of the conflict to another area where you hold the high ground, or move it to the middle ground; this will give them the impression that conflict is on a level playing field and may not lead to their definite defeat. If you are stuck and in doubt, pacify them. Do not be afraid to admit you were wrong – after all, this is the low ground. If you have nothing left to offer and the low ground is your domain, see the section 'Defence From Above'.

Mastering the low ground is as important as mastering any other ground because it is the staging area for larger conflicts. A Superior will ask an Inferior for their view on something simply because the Inferior is inexperienced, and in no position to source the knowledge they need, and because of these factors their reply will be the answer the Superior craves to prove *their* point to their Superior. The Inferior in the Low Ground may take a calculated risk on what little they know, but if their little piece of knowledge is found to be wrong, it will temporarily stain their career. Don't defend what you don't know.

Reality: Three words that can change your life: "I don't know."

Don't fight a battle if you don't gain anything by winning
– Erwin Rommel

Middle Ground – You All Know the Same

Like the pitched battlefields of World War One, this is where the most ferocious and prolonged duels take place. Two people, of equal standing on the one subject, need to prove their worth over the other; this is the protracted game of 'who knows the mostest about the middlest'. They will drag in allies from near and far, every inch of terrain will be showered not by blood but by saliva from the constant bickering. The outcome will probably be decided on a whim by someone in the high ground after a liquid lunch. Holding the middle ground is awkward; it can be attacked from above by ambitious fuckers, and cannon fodder, *en masse* and cheeky, from below. Middle ground is also the home of the motivated who wish to get somewhere, but have no desire to stomp on heads to get to the top. They are vulnerable to attack and character assassination, but because of the stability offered by positions of 'responsibility' characteristic of the middle ground, defence is the norm and it is fostered. If both warring parties are on the middle ground a truce needs to be called and an inventory of what is known or not known needs to be made. If all parties feel the venturing is too rough, hire someone to take the fall for a wrong decision. Again, speed dial the consultant to come in and deconstruct the problem, or delegate one of your minions to pull their hair out over it.

If you are entrenched in a middle ground duel to the death or unemployment office, do not dig yourself into a fortified position that you will die of embarrassment defending. Although the stakes are high, be flexible at all costs. Take your opposition's point of view, and make it your own. Give them a bit of what they want and take as much as you can from them. Confuse the situation until your opponent is worn out. There is nothing worse than a stalemate, so keep the lines of communication open and keep the action happening; exchange ideas and coded insults. Think of it as a dance – when the music's over – so is the fun. If this is your domain, read the section on 'Tactics' at least twice.

Example:

Jack and Jill have a team leader called Fatso. Fatso knows Jack and Jill's expertise so he routinely uses them as appropriate, until they get too comfortable and slack. Fatso wants to impress his piers and superiors, so he enlists Jack to win over senior management, which is something Jill sees herself as on the middle ground. Jack is at a disadvantage, and will face tough competition from Jill, who will be using all her cunning traits to prevent Jack from ever succeeding at winning over senior management. Why? Because if he does, Jill's expertise will diminish in everyone's eyes, and so will her responsibility and status. So she'll be out there winning over senior management too. At the same time, Fatso orders Jill to use her marketing and industry experience (her low ground) on a special high-profile project. At this point Jack sees Jill is approaching his middle ground, so he will set out to prove that he knows more about marketing and the industry. The winner? Fatso. Jack and Jill will be working harder, proving their worth. And Fatso's little team resembles a hive of dynamic activity. Come Friday, Fatso deserves a long lunch.

Make the host and the quest exchange places – Chinese Strategy

High Ground – You Know the Most

'Advantageous' rhymes with 'vicious'. If you want to conceptualise feuds on the high ground, think of knights in shining armour dropping their swords and chivalry and picking up machine guns. Do not venture into the high ground unless you can face the fury. Bluffers may slither from the low ground to the middle ground, but to reach the high ground is a different journey. The high ground is ringed by loyal middle ground defences that may act as though their positions are assailable, but nothing could be further from the truth – they will invite you in and cut you down. This intensity of these middle ground operators, orbiting like satellites around the high ground, makes the high ground all the more severe and un-approachable. It is the home of the artful courtesan, bred and educated to play sugary diplomacy with the sharpest of words as weapons. People devote careers to clawing their way up and attaining a high ground status and fending off pretenders whom they know very well because they used to be one.

Added to that is the paradox of accountability: those in the high ground in one area may be asked to comment on an area where they are in the low ground. Their superiority in one field is thought to transcend many others, so they must rely on some universal wisdom to please the crowd. This is how those in a high ground come to breach a low ground, and because few wish to expend themselves on defending the lower ground, so it is won over easily and repeatedly by those from above. Decisions are made by the wrong people, but this is nothing new, it is even fostered to the extent that those in the high ground must make the decisions because to attack them in return is next to impossible.

When you hold the high ground in knowledge do not explain everything to those in the low or middle ground. By explaining things they may not fully grasp you are implanting visions of equal knowledge which may come back to you in the form of an able competitor. If people seem to want to know, give them little portions to fulfil them but never fill them, turn them into an addict for something that only you control.

The supreme excellence is to subdue the armies of your enemies without even having to fight them – Sun Tzu

Defence from Above – Passing the Buck

When defending the low or middle ground, avoid becoming an object to be destroyed. Use what familiarity you have of the ground to surrender to the superior force and offer your services. Alternatively mirror their actions and avoid direct confrontation; retreat when they attack, advance when they retreat. Learn from them and one day you may follow them all the way to the pearly gates of the higher ground. If you are feeling brave and wish to fight out of the lower ground and prove your point, probe the aggressor for weaknesses and dance with them if need be. Do not risk a frontal attack, wait until they are at ease with your apparent weaknesses and then strike at their heart and move on. Heroics aside, the reality is much harsher. If an aggressor is out to get you and you have nowhere to run, memorise the following:

The Art of Office War Best Practice for Passing the Buck

Basically, light a fire and create a smoke screen followed by issuing emergency instructions.

The Smoke Screen: Gather information, cut it to pieces and re-assemble it with the flair of a seasoned abstract artist creating a collage. The goal is to create 'original' misinformation to alert and confuse the aggressor. If the risk is worth it, utilise outright, yet courageous, lies. Present them with something that will stop them dead in their tracks – the idea is to hold off you imminent obliteration.

The Emergency Instructions: The instructions must be easy to comprehend as the laminated, daft (and completely irrelevant when you're plummeting to earth) Evacuation Instructions found in the back of passenger seats on jet airplanes. Present to the aggressor, straight after the smoke screen, hints of the identity of someone or something that is really to blame (the aggressor blames you for something, they're after you, so shift this) and whilst maintaining perfect eye-contact with their glaring eyes, issue (false, perhaps?) directions to the 'real' holder of the infamous blame, rounded off with a few interesting accusations against a common enemy. Tiring and confusing your opponent is one thing, but you must give them an intriguing and satisfying decoy to chase and plunder. The task is to create the appearance that what they're after is in some domain other than yours.

It was kicked into the long grass – Civil Service Axiom

Defence from Below – With a Sledge Hammer

If anyone attacks you from below, determine what their true intention is. Some people crave the attention of jostling with high flyers, not for outright power or glory, but for intellectual entertainment or to prove to their own comrades that they are just that tiny bit superior, brave, or stubbornly stupid. People attack upwards in order to test defences, probe for weaknesses, gauge reaction timing, or simply to see how much you care about a particular issue. Defending from above can seem all fun and games until you realise that you are facing a threat. A threat is like an iceberg: all you see is the icy tip, pristine and pretty, sitting on the horizon. What you don't see is the invisible powerbase that gives it credibility, support, and buoyancy. Conflict is not fists and spears. In the digital age conflict involves the strategic use of knowledge to disprove the opposition, regardless of its credibility. Do this rapidly, without remorse, and because you can. But before you begin crushing their will, promote the opposite of what you are about to preach: invite comment, accept ridicule, sew the seeds of partial change, and then crush the rebellion in its infancy. Get to know the nature of the threat before dissecting it into digestible portions. When you are in power, stay there.

> *It is enough that the people know there was an election. The people who cast the votes decide nothing. The people who count the votes decide everything – Joseph Stalin*

Example:

Fatso, team leader extraordinaire, notices that Jack and Jill are beginning to suspect that they are being played off against each other. Jack and Jill now approach senior management separately, hinting that they could easily do Fatso's job. When word gets back to Fatso, he'll use his position to belittle Jack and Jill's respective strength and weaknesses. Kicking them far way from his high ground, he will say things like: 'Why can't you get your head around that?' 'Look what you did with that report!' 'We may have to get someone in who can do it better!' To prove his worth to senior management he'll set up something so that Jack and Jill are doomed – not so much to fail – but to show they're incapable of handling Fatso's job.

Power: Crushing Their Will

"... and then Jill met Tim from Marketing for some 1 on 1 networking tips and they hit it off like... "

Crushing Them for Fun

Bored? Frustrated? Want a bit of harmful fun? Then step out of yourself and momentarily ruin someone. It's not that hard to blow some aspect of their pride to bits. Follow it through with public introspection that leads to some degree of ridicule, but not something obvious that causes finger pointing and wagging at nasty old you. Just create some disturbance that gets people thinking. There are numerous tactics to adopt, but before you start utterly crushing their will, step back and consider exactly what you're doing. You can play nasty for fun, but it's just a useless charade unless you tie it to some goal, some greater plan that elevates you higher and higher, so you can prove to yourself and others that you are powerful.

Men would live exceedingly quiet if these two words, mine and thine, were taken away – Anaxagoras

The Dynamics of Power

The basics of power are: responsibility, accountability, status, security. They are all easy to say and preach until you *really* want to get somewhere. The fundamental behind humanity is will. I will do this. We must have that. If we can't get what we want, we will seek retribution. Translated for the contemporary times: will is power.

People crave power. In a perverse and diabolical way it's re-assuring to know your government and its allies have a nuclear arsenal. On the home front, power is the enraged pursuit of wealth. Money does bring happiness, so do simple pleasures; economic superiority over your environment is a comfort that is only human to pursue.

But power is like a stream; once it flows, it is un-stoppable and can turn into a river or a flood, until an act of nature banishes the source of water so it may spring somewhere else. You'll be left high and dry. You'll be devastated. You'll be like everyone else, clinging to someone else or the collective to feel a bit of power. This is the lifecycle of an office.

Power is not a monolithic entity; power by nature must compete with other powers and in doing so become sharper. Stalin relentlessly purged the best of his ranks to annihilate the mere hint of competition. Another drawback of power is that in order to keep it, you must learn more about yourself and distrust people you have always known. You have to consult people who don't know you, even enemies who despise you. Seek alternative answers. Challenge someone's expertise and see how they wield their knowledge as a tool of power. Experience how it feels to have power torching your face. The best thing to know about real power and not some self-help hypnosis is that it is up to you to moderate yourself. With this comes an extra-sensory responsibility: you are no longer simply aware of your basic needs, you are aware of everything and everyone that matters.

Reality: Even those with the most limited aspirations have to utilise elements of power to cruise their way through life. Some people appear to be born under a lucky star, but are calculating their every move because they are fraught with a fear of failure. Some people are doomed to failure. Everyone has a will and that is their field of power.

I know I'm an object of criticism in the world, but if I am being talked about, I must be doing the right thing – Kim Jong-il

No Power without Pain

There is no such thing as power without pain. Some may say power can be gained without pain but that's a painful concept in itself – how can power, using and coercing others, and filling hearts with notions of happiness not hurt? Indeed, power is the ability to make people believe they are doing something they like when they don't, so sooner or later there will be a feeling of pain. Even the guilt of knowing that you are using someone is a pain, so power is also about how you handle that pain. The first casualty of power will be you.

Name drop some of the most powerful figures in history and they will be synonymous with some of the worst vices of humanity: greed, jealousy, caprice, a hint of sadism. Were they that concerned with their less than desirable traits? If Alexander the Great wept because there were no more worlds to conquer, was he remorseful of those he squashed on the way? Do these things matter when all you want is just enough power to fortify your position and be happy? If you feel no pain with power, don't worry, it'll settle in afterwards and then you'll feel nothing at all. Get ready.

Heart, Action and Endeavour

There are many opinions regarding the accumulation of power, the use of strategy, and the paths to riches. By reading them you may feel as though you have embarked on a journey of a thousand miles with a single step. The journey *is* the destination, but in reality there *is* no end. Once you dedicate yourself to changing, you are forever changed. What determines the destination and the journey is your ability to focus not on what you wish to be (a dangerous and fanciful act) and to dissect exactly what you are, where you have been, what your weaknesses are, and how you can turn them into strengths. Once you know who you are and have an idea of where you are going, you have to pick a point on a virtual map of where you have to go, plot a path, and just do it. As always there are infinite options and the standard two are: do you follow the flock or make your journey alone on the road less travelled? These are decisions that no wisdom can prepare you for, because the decision is brutally and bluntly yours alone. Do you have the Heart? Can you live with yourself afterwards?

Once you believe you can, or you have no other choice (which is quite handy for deciding your fate), you need action.

Action is the most misused and misunderstood term for 'doing things'. What is action, what is laziness, what constitutes a piecemeal effort to please some inspirational cloud in your mind? Once again, if your heart is not in it, then your action won't be. You may trick yourself that you are attempting something out of your league, but you probably aren't. If you are resolved to take action, but are unsure, (maybe you are set back by doubt, first failures, ridicule) the best way to know you are getting somewhere is the blinding experience of an incredible delightful pain – discovery. In one moment you will feel a great aching in the mind followed by a heartbreaking revelation. All that you may have believed will be swept aside, and this is a cause of pain, but pain that represents growth and healing. If you're not facing up to what you always thought you knew and trusted, then you are most likely going nowhere. But don't wish for the pain of discovery, don't encounter a little of that pain and amaze yourself at your bravery for pulling through. If you really want to do something you have to take it all the way.

Heart is the ignition, action is the acceleration, but endeavour is the vehicle that will show you what you always had but never recognised. From there it is on to the stars.

Alas, all of the above is half the story. Now that you are on the way somewhere, the excitement begins.

Building a Powerbase

A powerbase is envied; if it is not envied, it is worthless. Although you may have the best intentions for your little powerbase, if it is not feared then it is powerless. Therefore, your powerbase needs teeth, fury, mobility, leadership, and camouflage. In the context of the office this translates to varied yet co-existing ingredients:

You need *access to information* across all spectrums and the means to interpret and manipulate information for your own advantage. Because information is a currency, horde it like a bank, lend it out a premium, but most importantly, keep it flowing. The stagnation of information in any system spells death.

You need *intelligent and focussed people*, an obvious statement, yet who really gets the people they really want? Someone that was great for the last year and up until yesterday might be tired today, and thinking about changing careers tomorrow; getting a better paid job or position, or moving to the country for next summer. You have no control over people, particularly intelligent people.

Get people for what they want to do. While some people are drones, others are battle-axes, who cares when all you want is a geek to cut code? Have someone with people skills, and if you can't find anyone, be that person. Get your people working for you and you do the communication with other powerbases. Most people just want to do their task, become engrossed, and excel. Their devotion leads to reward and these people want to be managed. Let people be what they want.

Mobility, the ability to shift, duck, jump and attack. Many powerbases are entrenched in a mono-dimensional struggle, and the more energy they invest in it, the more they see it as a titanic struggle. It may be their function to take on such tasks, but it will be their end if they can't perform on other fronts. A powerbase must be able to adapt to new situations, reverse failure, divert flak, interpret criticism, and recover lost ground. Mobility also means shape shifting and deploying itself to take advantage of a new situation. More about this later.

Synergy within Unity. A successful powerbase is a robust ecosystem. On the outside it looks set and stable, but on the inside it is alive and buzzing. It could be transported to an alien environment and thrive.

The Work Ethic of the Leader. Whoever is in charge must lead by example without becoming a workaholic success-driven maniac. The leader must have an inner balance before they can lead and expect to balance the diverse nature of people that make up their powerbase. There are numerous management styles for all sorts of situations so let's keep it really simple: A leader should be firm and down-to-earth, confident in their own ability and the ability of those around them. This is what wins the day. Anyone can be a leader, but people who enjoy leading will move the mountains.

Part of the problem in building a powerbase, or re-generating one, is that it must be tiered with an overall *strategy*. The flexibility of the leader when upgrading the powerbase and altering strategy to suit the surrounding and future environments is what makes them successful.

You may despair as you read this, because you don't have a powerbase, are not part of one, and may never have one. A powerbase doesn't have to be formally recognised, it can be just as dangerous as an informal social net, free from the constraints of protocol. Your powerbase can consist of your colleagues and friends, united by a common exclusion from existing powerbases.

Alternatively, your powerbase might be you: your skills, your drive, your intellect, your knowledge; all of which is yours to capitalise on.

> *Nothing can have value without being an object of utility*
> *– Karl Marx*

Strategy

A Very Strategic Introduction

A strategy is relative to the environment it is to be applied. While there are a thousand books on strategy and you may have a strategy to read them all, they won't help because strategy is not fixed. Yes, some things remain the same like dull walls, middle-aged paunches, and continental drift, but the crux of strategy is about being in the right place at the right time with the right means to get what you want. So much can be said about it, but it may not help you directly. The most effective help for the beginner, the in-experienced, the dreamers or the frustrated, is to give them a kick up the arse.

Great ability develops and reveals itself increasingly with every new assignment – Baltasar Gracian

Failing to Plan

Most people prove their strategic intellect by identifying strategic failure. They point out the lack of focus, initiative, the fact that it is too fast or too slow, too this, too anything, too much and not enough. The detractor makes strategic success un-obtainable, but if something does happen that was strategic and successful, they strategically play up to it as something that happened from 'above' and was bound to happen. Before understanding strategy, you have to understand how people refute it, and how to ignore them. If people sniff a strategy, they will oppose it even when they can't forecast the outcome. There will always be those who will throw up barriers to strategy. Fear of change is hardwired into the brain; it is closely followed by envy of others' better ideas. If they beg for attention and warn you against your strategy, give the detractor as much credit as they need, because if you fail they can become an ally and shoulder to cry on – after all, they knew all along. And should you succeed, the look on their faces is an experience best enjoyed in reality. If you can't stand them then just ignore them completely – don't complain to them, and certainly don't explain to them.

Pure Convictions

The comfort that oozes from the ergonomic normality and gentleness of an office is a pacifying strategy; you're there to relax and focus on the job at hand. Many a great inventor has worked from a dingy shed and gone on to world class laboratories, but the air-conditioned office that is comfortable enough to work in and indulge in balanced social interaction, deprives most passive people of reasons to rise above their duty. Active people, the ambitious, the driven and the maniacs, have their own reasons, which are usually something personal, to focus and drive them forward. And those that succeed have a strategy. For the passive, their strategy is to remain passively in place but aligned with the greater strategy, to keep the show on the road, the boss happy, and their own employment guaranteed. For the active, their strategy is to prosper.

Defining a personal strategy and acting it out is easy in principle, much like a diet after a holiday, but there has to be a certain predetermined destination. You need tangible points to gauge the effective implementation of your strategy. And to really do this you need a conviction. A strategic conviction is something you cannot neglect because it is part of you – it is your inescapable and private motivation. Strategies are based on a person's basic requirements: they want a promotion for more pay to buy a bigger house for their growing family. This is very middle class, very broad, and the most popular conviction in the office, because who wants to bring up a family in a shoe-box?

Strategy and the implementation of it, is also reliant on what physically exists. Man could not walk on the moon if the moon wasn't there, and man could not even attempt to smash into the moon without a succession of nasty wars and tinkering scientists to develop rocket technology. A common mistake in strategic thinking is to assume everything is at their fingertips. People may be modest in what they wish for, but in reality they will never get anywhere on wishful thinking alone. Strategic thinking is based on observing what is actually out there, where you want to go, whether it is possible, and adapting to the nature of the journey. Once you know your strategy and why you are acting it out, you can begin to utilise, experiment and enjoy deploying tactics to navigate that journey.

> *Convictions are more dangerous foes of truth than lies*
> *– Friedrich Nietzsche*

Addicted to Outcomes – Give It Up

Again, more sobering up before your drunken Strategy Spree that leads to your glorious crowning over kingdoms and riches and harems, or more painfully, a debt-ridden department in a corporate shoe-box populated by slackers.

The light at the end of the tunnel for Strategy is the Outcome. One of the greatest flaws in modern industrial thinking has been the addiction to the Outcome; it may take ten years to build a worthwhile machine (i.e., a new car, a solar panel to meet a home's energy needs, a new hair-dryer) for the people but after a decade, peoples' needs have changed. The Outcome might have worked in the past but it won't work in the now. Furthermore, in office life, where accountability and conformity rule the day, what people agree on (usually through a path of least resistance, therefore an average punt) as the Outcome is what they may be tying their career to. Now the Outcome, instead of a guiding light, becomes a blinding light because if it fails and goes out, so do they. Never be afraid to shift the Outcome and the Strategy.

> *Belief and seeing are both often wrong... Be prepared to*
> *re-examine your reasoning – Robert Strange McNamara*

Tactics

Tactically Speaking

Before using the following tactics for your own gain, you need to understand how these tactics have been used against you. Remember the tactics that affected you and how they either altered or squashed you? What was the outcome? Would you do the same in retaliation? What is it all for? When adopting tactics, use discretion and structure them to an overall strategy. Don't waste your time and energy trying to prove your fangs are venomous – just get on with it and take a delicious bite.

The Pecking Order or the Chain of Command

The pecking order is the structured, rational and lawful way of doing things, much like a tablet of commandments for religious folk. People know where they are on the ladder, where their superiors, inferiors, sworn enemies, and competitors are on the mighty chain of command chart. And you know where they all should rightly be if you had your way. The beginner has the belief that their reward for hard work, commitment and playing the game is progression up the ladder. But sadly, the pecking order is really only an induction presentation illustration used by over enthusiastic human resources staff on new recruits. The pecking order exists as a structure for all to admire but in reality is a flimsy cardboard cut out.

Behind the facade is the power play of diplomatic favouritism and professional preference, the push and pull of interpersonal cohesion based on sex (or flirtatious desires), shared attitude and interest, and of course envy and any other frail human trait that seeps into the foray. Nothing is what it seems; the pecking order is not misused or used, because the real powers at play work in their own way. Once you break the charade and investigate what really happens and why, you can get lost in trying to understand why an organisation works the way it does. Once these powers have had their play, you'll notice a change in the pecking order. Set out as a diagram you'll see who has switched places, but it'll never tell you *why*. It's best to come to accept that people are elevated all the time to positions they don't deserve. When is it your turn?

Misusing Group Dynamics

When someone says 'we are dynamic', think of team work, collaboration, feuding and rubbery reconciliation. If the pecking order represents the secret polarity of people, group dynamics is the weather system of the company.

.... Likes	– – – – Dislikes	———— Passionate Dislike

These invisible forces are at play, and once you understand them beyond their face value, you are able to determine why inter-departmental relationships have gone sour, and you can begin to use them for your own advantage. It will be the personalities within the group that are the root cause, so keep in mind that by forming allegiances with one, you will be creating an enemy from another. Group dynamics is about how well people and their respective groups within the main body work or don't work; it is in permanent flux and is not a force that can be shaped by any one individual unless they are the outright ruler. The interplay of personalities, the obliging staff, the fertile minds of new staff and stubbornness of old-timers are not hindrances either, they are resources. As a ship sails on the wind you will go nowhere without shared resentment, perfectly undue favouritism, and allegiances.

Working the System

On the outside people appear to be playing their part and working with the system for the benefit of the organisation. In reality they are working the system – everyone has their own idea how to get ahead as fast as possible and with as least grief as possible. What people have as their strategy to working the system is their strength and weakness. Find these out and use them against them. The best way to find their strategy is to look at their personal life and how it fits in with their work life. There will be talk of a work/life balance but in reality, when someone has a paltry waged income, it is their personal life that takes precedence and determines how *they* work the system, regardless of how much they boast that they may be the world's number one workaholic. The job will serve their lifestyle and realistically – so what?

For the more motivated, working the system involves working everyone around them into the ground for their selfish purposes, and thus carving up a larger piece of the prize for their deep little pockets. As mentioned before, the secretive power play in un-official factions, groups of friends and 'teams' is fertile soil for someone to work the system. Who likes who, who hates you, who do you like, is it a personality or professional egotistical clash? Take advantage of these relationships, because although they are not documented as part of the schematics of the organisation, they are lubricants in the machine. Get people working off one another. Create rivalries that serve you. Look around, and identify where it has already happened, and who profits. And don't be alarmed.

The system, like mankind tinkering with nature, cries out to be worked. To work the system, do not completely alter your behaviour to suit. By all means fit in to the system, but let the system absorb you. Then you can begin to implement actions that enable you to work it. It's easier on the inside than out, and concentrate on the long term.

Do not be afraid to jump at advantageous offers, and as you satisfy your own needs, never pity the fruitless endeavours of the hapless opposition. Eradicate pity from your approach to the office unless you have to cry crocodile tears over some fool's early departure. Few work the system without causing some degree of mayhem and discomfort so get used to it.

Timing, Speed, Accuracy & Deliberate Misses

There is a beat to life, like a waltz, and pressing your ear to the wall, or dance floor, keeps you abreast of where the dancers are at. Before embarking on a deed with timing, speed and accuracy in mind, think about the necessity of the deed and whether you have the guts. Many people know a strategy, play out a tactic in their mind, know the right time and where to aim but fall at the point of initiation – they can't go through with the deed because they fear the reprisal. Fear will in turn affect timing, speed and accuracy, thereby causing a seemingly deliberate miss; an ill-aimed throw that alerts your competition to danger and incites them to a speedy revenge. In order to have timing, speed and accuracy, be brave about your business, become fearless, and if all else fails, use your new talents to throw up a flurry of excuses.

He who fears being conquered is sure of defeat
– Napoleon Bonaparte

Mobility

First and foremost is the ability to change. You cannot change your backbone but you can change your method of defending it. In the office you can't exactly duck and run from your active duties (though many do and make a career out of it), so mobility is applied to how you deal with the currency of the office – knowledge. Be malleable about the points of view, methods and tactics that you will have to use in the future. Do not discredit anything outright. Do not have complete faith in the ways of the past. Do not expect and respect too much. Give yourself latitude, a free space to manoeuvre, should the need arise.

Mobility also extends to awakening those around you to a threat. Mobility is also about motivating people to work for, or with you, against a threat that may affect all of you even though many do not care for you. In the final analysis, mobility is motivation.

Mobility is also a contradiction – you are a slippery pole that none can climb, yet simultaneously a rock for people to rely on. You need to be both at the same time and use the one senile customer-service smile. You have to be fixed somewhere, otherwise all the moving and flexing creates the impression that you are fixed to nothing but a lot of hot air. So now you need to determine what you should be fixed on, and what you should be fluid about. Sounds hard and ridiculous? Well, nearly. To get around it all, be what people want you to be, based on what they need, what they think is of value, and what is not.

Observation

Again, the clichés: due-diligence, effective listening, itemisation, risk-assessment, (using) emotional intelligence. Why is plain old 'observation', the art of looking around you and seeing what is going on, re-invented by consultants, re-branded and labelled a valuable tool, and deemed indispensable to the running of the office? The fact that it is explained as a procedure we should all follow with an acute sense of purpose is proof that everywhere, everyday, people aren't really observing, and some people are smart enough to get paid to tell people what they should be doing all along: Observing. Why can't people just observe, why the need to be sold it and told it? Sadly, people, in their usual slack way, observe only what is necessary. Everything else lies in their periphery and falls into the 'not my concern' category.

But people who are out to get what they want observe with a keener eye and ear. They don't make a point of observing and carrying out their own due-diligence, perfecting effective listening and itemisation, carrying out risk-assessment or harnessing emotional intelligence, all at their own expense of time and energy, because what they learn becomes their property and they translate it into the terrain they'll have to master and travel across to get what they want. Observation becomes relative to where you're going. Know your Enemy. Empathise with the Devil.

Motivation

Getting people motivated sounds great. So does 'thinking positive'. How about 'being proactive' and 'the glass is half-full, not half-empty'. Mention any of these infuriating over-used clichés, and your colleague will obligingly reply, 'Great! When do we start'?' but will do the exact opposite.

Undue calls for motivation make people feel like morons, so do not attempt to motivate anyone unless it is based on a feasible opportunity. Yes, take risks, but don't misuse 'motivation' for effect. Save it for action. Tie motivation to conviction – make them behave like horses neck and neck, in a race.

If you have to play the part and act motivated to impress the sad clowns at the top, perfect some ailment of *over* motivation; be too enthusiastic about pointless activities and perfect a 'glazed over' look of amazement 'just to be here'. Ask the key motivators if they're as motivated as you. Turn 'buzz' into brinkmanship, "I'm more motivated than you, shithead." Soon motivation will climax into an exasperated cry (because motivation, like drama, must peak and dissipate) followed by a dull sigh. Now you can get back to normal.

> *It's not hard to make decisions when you know*
> *what your values are – Roy Disney*

How to Win a Debate and Prove a Point

The key to successful debating is recognising the innate human desire to know not just facts, but plausible stories that lead to the fact. The fact, or what you prove to be fact, can be what the hell you like, as long as you build the case, through a story, for its existence. There is symmetry here, so you can't have one without the other, and neither should one outweigh the other. Because a debate must appear to rely on wholly credible points it is actually easy to construct a story – the debate is set within the framework of the truth. By linking the points of truth and highlighting their importance as you progress your story – implanting your point of view – you win the debate. It also helps if you believe what you're saying, because by the time you have won the debate, you will be expected to act upon your stated position or you'll never be taken seriously.

To counteract a masterful debater you must identify their key point and its validity then discredit it. Throw your opponent off their centre of balance just as you would in a wrestling match. Do not waste time with basic and easy scoring – aim for the guts of where they are heading. Pre-empt (you may know) what their final point will be, how they will get there, and get there first. Steal their wind, agree on their point (at least partially) and then embed it in a story. Turn that story around and lead it to disaster. If there's an audience, entertain them.

Play Their Game on Your Terrain

You foresee the trajectory of your adversary. You cannot know their every move or how fate will intervene, but what you can count on is the existence of an opposing strategy that is probably designed to deal with you. Knowing your opposition is one thing, and entering into conflict is another, but doing it on your terrain is infinitely preferable. Try to enter their terrain, familiarise yourself with it, then understand where they are coming from and how they would attack you. Now step back into your terrain and invite them in.

Character Assassination and the Backstab

The best approach is indirect. Let others do your work for you. Say you are A, you detest C, and B is unwittingly a mediator for everyone. Don't tell B about your fanatical observations about C, go to D, who will tell E, who will tell B, who will then mistrust C. In order to poison someone you need to highlight a truth which gives rise to a lie. Start with the truth, add the lie, and let it roll. Use gossip and patience, and watch your defamatory words spread, prosper and fester. Sometimes it can go completely out of hand and develop along lines that you could not anticipate, but this is part of the risk. Sometimes to implant a lie you need to halve it and tell one half to one person, the other half to another, knowing full well that they will exchange gossip and do something exciting and titillating – add your half and your other half together and get *their* one. Now they will think they are information superior and waste no time exploiting this for their own gain. But in reality, it is your gain.

If you suspect you are on the receiving end of such malice and you don't know where it originated from, become an irresistible target. Play a bit naïve for a while, a bit silly, a bit deserving of a public thrashing, so that your enemies have the cheap and arrogant cheekiness to rise and go for an easy shot. Take the shot on the chin. Have something to strike immediately back at them.

When you suspect someone is digging the knife in your back but can't be sure, be extra nice to them. If they have been extra nasty to you, they'll be extra nice now to compensate. Because they know they have wronged you, it will make them feel uneasy to see that you really are not that bad, or a threat, after all. This is the calm in the eye of the storm and a defining moment: it is the declaration of *civil* office war. Once you know who and how nasty they really are, hold your tongue. Start your own campaign.

> *The tongue is like a sharp knife...*
> *Kills without drawing blood – Buddha*

Sidelining

Sidelining occurs when the victim is effectively cut off from the main group but is not spurned in the same way as a leper. People sideline people in order to remove them because the victim is either a threat or a waste of space. How sidelining occurs is simple:

The victim is no longer invited to participate in group events. Group events can be anything, but a good way to start sidelining is to politely exclude them from trivial group events that they aren't interested in anyway. By the time the group event evolves into something important for all concerned (its true intention) it's too late for the victim to rejoin it.

Now the victim is outside the group and faces an insurmountable task not unlike an individual trying to sway a faction. They are isolated, but want to be part of the group.

If the victim genuinely wants to rejoin the group, then they can of course kowtow to the group's ways. Some groups like people to bend to their ways as a sign of commitment.

Sidelining in an office is rife because of the personalities, politics, and plain business interests. The goal of sidelining is to deny the victim the right to participate in a decision making process and prohibit them from accessing certain knowledge they could profit from. Because offices are complex places and bureaucracy madness, like nature flourishing in a vacuum, thrives in an atmosphere of jealousy and superstition, victims can join little informal factions, thereby legitimising themselves, and being part of their own group, create a powerbase. Soon there are groups against groups, and groups sidelining other groups, all with the purpose of denying others decision making rights and access to knowledge. At this point, a manager will have to pick up the axe and carve things back into place. Groups may be broken apart but allegiances will remain strong. Sidelining will continue on a psychological level. The only way to deal with this is to actually remove people.

Isolation

Gulags, prisons, the threat of Hell, are all forms of isolation that sit heavily in our minds. Everybody has the same weakness – we need social interaction, we need to be understood, we need to be valued, and we strive to be in pleasant environments. Isolation is the next logical step after sidelining whereby the victim is starved of all human creature comforts. If you want to isolate someone approach the people they communicate the most with. Start with someone who is easily swayed and poison their minds about the person you wish to isolate. Then move on to the next, and the next. Quietly and politely hound them out the door.

Poisoning Knowledge

People are not very easily corruptible, so only the truly wicked are adept at poisoning knowledge for their own purpose. Thanks to the civil nature of the office, and its reliance on knowledge, poisoning can be used to refute a competitor's worth. It is part of conflict and is very simple: knowledge is poisoned by discrediting its purpose, methods of creation, and output. So we might ask, 'Why are you doing that? It was never supposed to be like that; it will never go anywhere'. The end result is the removal of a competitor's responsibility.

The poisoning can be subtle, and can even involve minimal discrediting. It is not a direct personal attack; it is the best type of personal attack, because an employee's worth is discredited on a 'rational' basis rather than emotional vindictiveness. They feel worthless.

If you suspect someone is out to poison the knowledge you are working on, observe how they communicate with the person who pays for your output. At some point, the person who finances your 'flawed' knowledge will have to gauge what is real and what is rubbish. As for the perpetrator, do not challenge them; monitor what they're working on and where they wish to head. Find out what part of their employment means a lot to them, but don't poison that yet. Use the pain of flattery first.

The Pain of Flattery

Flattery gets some people everywhere; some are full of tardy praise to cloak their broken promises, some use it wisely to gain favour. You can flatter people sparingly, a little bit here and there, or it may be your forte in life, but to be on the receiving end, beyond what is actually deserving, is courting and postponing a moment of failure. Flattery raises expectations and if you can't meet or surpass these expectation then you'll be facing your little Waterloo.

Beware people who flatter and praise too much. They may do it out of gratitude, kindness, or sincerity, but isn't that their greatest weapon? Remember that all the energy expended on praising you, or even a miserly amount, could just as well been used to scorn you.

He who knows how to flatter also knows how to slander
– Napoleon Bonaparte

Repression

Repression of competition by any means enables the repressor to hold their ground when attacked from people below. One day they may wish to move up, or they may have encountered a brick wall or glass ceiling, but they know where they are and they don't want You rising up to their level and beyond. Therefore, to stay perched at a career pinnacle, a Repressor will repress all those around them and below, in any way, so they can remain in their own position indefinitely.

The old adage that people rise to their level of incompetence and stay there refers to the art of repression: you can see this trait in Repressors who are in positions they deem important on the inside, and yet you perceive them as typecast bumbling fools. You and someone else may be in competition for a promotion, but under the artful eye of the Repressor the weaker one will be promoted because if the smart one were, one day they might topple the Repressor from their high ground. Once someone who is weak is promoted, they will forever be in debt to the Repressor. In repressive environments, most may barely survive, but the weak positively prosper.

Once a Repressor sits on their little throne and has implemented a neat strategy to monitor its subjects and keep them at arms reach, the Repressor makes grand claims about the throne being available to 'everyone'. Then they promote the weak, the idiots, and watch them fall into public humility. The Repressor has then proved that in fact the throne is not just for everyone, but for a special someone – them. They instil awe, unwarranted though it may be, but that is their survival tactic.

Divide and conquer – Roman proverb

Bullying

Bullying, or being plain mean and nasty for the hell of it, is partially accidental. Some people are bullies by their nature, whereas others stand up to bullying, and some people even get off on the interaction. Generally speaking, bullying is purposefully used as a blunt form of coercion. So instead of some flowery person anointing niceties on you and requesting that you partake in activity A, the bully makes life so unbearably hard and paints activity A as the only solution to find peace, so you jump at it. The bonus is you are aware that you're jumping to activity A, rather than having your mind bent, or sucking up the niceties from that flowery someone. Nonetheless, the bully and the flowery person both want you to do something. Usually it's all for their benefit, not yours, which is why you're forced or tricked into it. There's not much you can do with a bully, particularly if your income relies on them, but you can bully them back. If a dog snarls at you, snarl back.

Serial Incompetence

Insanity is doing the same thing over and over again, and expecting a different outcome each time. Serial incompetence is the acceptance of incompetence, for an unfathomable gain. Serial incompetents in the office resemble the products of spooky evolution that take place on an isolated island divorced from mainland savagery. There creatures evolve in peculiar environments; give them tropical sunshine, a rock to lie on, a sea brimming with easy prey, and you can end up with very lazy creatures. In human form, the creatures have more leeway – not only do they live, but they make mistakes, lazing their days away on the cushion of a society floating in a sea of excess that tolerates their mistakes. Serial incompetents are at the far end of the 80% cannon fodder spectrum, they are the exemplars of how wrong anti-ambition can go. They are deluded, they are happy, they are everywhere. But they do serve a purpose other than being models of low, zero, or negative production. They are the ones who can disrupt the plans of the ambitious.

Example

Your Rival implants the idea in your Boss's head that a certain Serial Incompetent should team up with You. It all seems very honourable – the Incompetent may learn a thing or two from You. When the moment comes you realise You cannot teach the Incompetent anything. Furthermore they can not help You, and the more You have to help Them the more ground your Rival has made on You. Your Boss now thinks You can't manage someone simple like the Serial Incompetent (your Boss might even begin formulating a devious plan to transfer incompetent You to a rival Boss's team). So devise a plan whereby whatever You and the Incompetent were working on has to be given up, so the fruitless partnership peels apart and the Serial Incompetent is sent packing to some other domain. Create some face saving excuse for the Serial Incompetent to please the crowd. No matter how you get out of the situation, You have lost time, your Rival is ahead, and the last your Boss thinks of You is Incompetence. The Serial Incompetent is as always, happy to help, or appears to be.

Another example of Serial Incompetence is something less publicised buy widely active: if a superior can not fire, cast-away or drown the Serial Incompetent, then they may just have to promote them out. The Serial Incompetent is set up with a little role, probably more ceremonial than practical, out of harm's way.

Hell is the impossibility of reason – Dante

Bribery

Everyone has their price, and if you don't believe it just look at your pay cheque: you have been bribed to perform a service. Some people jump through hoops of fire, some people scrub toilets, some people fly into space, but you have been bribed to bide your time in an office. Bribery is so far reaching that the law will never keep up with it. Besides, bribery is so tainted with its cousin 'corruption' that they easily get confused and legislated for or against. Bribes take many forms and mean many things: sometimes they appear as rewards, sometimes as the only real payment you'll ever see. If you are setting out to bribe someone, don't insult them, make it really obvious. Bribes are the cornerstone of civilisation, so don't be afraid to add a sweetener in order to get what you want. Who knows what barbaric state the 3rd Millennium would be without civilised, institutional and reward-based bribery through the ages?

Childish Antics

Throw a tantrum, break something useless (a pen, an old chair, a mug), huff and puff and sulk, complain until you're red in the face and an audience is sinking with pity. Pull out cables from networks, spit out hot coffee onto the carpet, stamp your feet. You know you want to, and when you do, you know it might just work. Of course the success of childish antics in a grown-up working environment are relative to the personalities involved, but when it does work it's because of this: Those who have no shame in stooping so low and base do so because everyone else is afraid of them; when people witness childish antics, they are embarrassed (some are a bit envious too) and wish it to stop and the only way that seems to work is to cater to the child. Give it the candy. Shut it up because it's killing us.

When faced with someone resorting to childish tactics, never speak to them like a parent, or worse a child, all in the name of 'connecting', thus trying to play their game. Be an adult, be stern, it's a game of nerves, and like all children, sooner or later the child will change tactics or need a good lie-down. If people get away with Childish Antics, then everyone will resort to it, so repress it as soon as possible.

Forgiveness

Some do, some don't. There is nothing more annoying than someone who has deceived you, and is now pleading with you to forgive them, all puppy-dog-eyed and preying on your better nature. See how easily you submit to their will, see how easily you become weaker, and see how easily you feel like the one that has done wrong. Feel the resentment of forgiveness.

An act of clemency may be an act of grace, but at the opposite end of the social pact, a plea for forgiveness could be an indicator that someone is out to double-deceive you. Never forget those you have to forgive, because after you're forgiven them they'll most likely think of you as an easy pushover.

Revenge (served cold)

Revenge is a dish best served cold, but if you plan to serve revenge as a hot dish, use an oven and not a microwave, and don't stay around for dessert. A 'cold revenge' is to increase its severity. It is on 'a dish' because the receiver has to swallow it. As for you – the deceiving fool bent on revenge – you have two options: do you want to be held in high regard for your action, or do you wish all to know they have suffered and you have not and now you can sleep easier? If you put yourself into the limelight as the one who took revenge, you are shifting your role from artful avenger to big fat target ready to stew in your own juices. This will be your downfall, so prepare to digest your cold self.

If you wish to have no fame for your revenge, you are playing a strategic game that will prove to people who suspect it was you that you really mean business. And if you never claim responsibility when everyone knows what you have done, then your reputation is set: you are scary.

A man that studieth revenge keeps his own wounds green
– Francis Bacon

The Unpredictable

Being unpredictable in an office is like placing a child with the plague in a nursery. The gatekeepers of both rigidly controlled environments will try their hardest to exclude the plagued unpredictable individual. Nonetheless when they do get in they prosper. The child gives the plague to its new friends and the plague wins. The unpredictable individual can create instability by disrupting the *status quo* once they have tricked their way into the office. Offices hire predictable people in the hope that they are too dumb to do anything other than their required menial tasks, and not something unpredictable like start their own enterprise in direct competition with the hand that fed them. But being unpredictable is important on a subversive level: when no one knows what you are really capable of then they will be less inclined to take advantage of you.

There are no formulae to being unpredictable or creative methods in the execution of it, and it is definitely not the type of trait to wear on your sleeve. You may think taking different routes from A to B is just the start, or breaking free from the established process and forming your own style is cool and innovative, but unpredictable actions must at some point lead to a profitable outcome otherwise people will think of you as a maniac. The art of unpredictability is to make what you're doing appear so sudden and effortless, so obviously different, and above all successful. Your adversaries must be in awe of your unpredictability. Don't tell anyone what you are really doing. But by all means drop hints of what is to come to create the impression of foresight.

Remember: people will believe anything when they are in a vacuum and praying for truth. Provide whatever it is, unpredictably, and they will think of you as a miracle worker.

You win battles by knowing the enemy's timing, and using a timing which the enemy does not expect – Miyamoto Musashi

Reputation

Everyone has a reputation that is hard to shake, but once eradicated you can re-mould yourself. If you are happy with your reputation (new, old, or the only one you've ever had) you must protect, nurture, and carry it. If you have not done so already, become the reputation you wish to be. Use it sparingly and wisely, as a force that precedes the real you so that it inspires people to do great things and crushes people who get in your way. Never be too modest about your reputation, balance it with a believable flaw. Let your competition know of this weakness; it could be something symbolic to them but purely base and idiotic to you, so that when they start to attack you can detect them from miles away thinking they're pushing your buttons.

A horse is a thing of beauty... none will tire of looking at him as long as he displays himself in his splendour – Xenophon

Intentions – Nobody Knows What is Going On

Yes, it's a state of mind, and sadly, a state of the state. In this age of accountability the evidence of actions is written in data. People are held to account longer and longer, perhaps for as long as humans rely on data. People as ever are reticent to boast of their next nasty move. It is better to plan, move into position, and take action on a small scale for something of personal benefit than to hold a focus group to highlight problems and deficiencies, spread doubt, warn your competitors, and then stumble into a trap. While it is admirable to keep your intentions to yourself, you should work out how to understand others' intentions by listening to what they do and don't say. Learn how to hold your intentions secret until it is too late for the competition.

Pre-empt your next competitor's intentions by clarifying what they are reticent to say.

Attempt easy tasks as if they were difficult, and difficult as if they were easy; in the one case that confidence may not fall asleep, in the other that it may not be dismayed – Baltasar Gracian

Being There and Not

This is the simplest and most subtle of tricks that anger people, but should not be taken out of context. A bureaucratic machine does not ignore your request for action out of contempt. Yes they despise you, but they are lazy, they have a presence to uphold so to move expediently for you may set an example they could never sustain. On a one-to-one basis, waiting for a reply, and waiting, don't take the bait. Don't be angered by delay, because it gives you time to think of every possible reply, as well as how to demand more. On the other hand, an excellent tactic is to reply yourself well before the time you specified. You surprise the receiver into submitting to what they may not have had time to expect or predict.

Another way to 'be there and not' is to not be there when you should be, and have some great excuse. Taking a sick day and arousing interest in your well being, works to your advantage and makes others wait for your return. This trick is not to be misused though. It is an ace up your sleeve, unless of course, you are chronically fatigued.

Let Your Superior be Superior

Although you know that your superior has risen to their 'personal best yet' level of incompetence, this is not an invitation to prove your incompetence by trying to match or even surpass them. What they want from you is diligence and hard work, and these you will provide, with some much favoured added-extras; you will ask questions that belie your naivety on some subjects, while displaying genius in others. There is a balancing act at play, because you are a student and your superior, the teacher, feels satisfied and secure in the knowledge that you are on the eternal quest for knowledge and yet you will never graduate to anything greater than them. And if you feel you know a way of doing things better, don't tell them your best ideas, give them clues, flesh it out a little, and let them take the lead and implement it. This is all fine and dandy except that should your seed idea flourish into a flower, your superior takes the credit. If it all turns to weeds, you'll take the blame. But what does that matter? After all, you are on learning curve.

There are three ways to think of your superior:

1. They are there to be ousted and one day I will be in their place.

2. They are there to be disposed of and replaced by someone better, but not me.

3. They are there, genius or fool that they are, and I can get on with my job without too much interference from them.

Don't try to better them; they will only have to squash you to maintain their own confidence in their position.

To equal a predecessor, one must have twice they worth
– Baltasar Gracian

Be the Fool, Pacifist, Dragon, Princess, or Knight

Loosely fixed to the official pecking order and chain of command is a non-official code of conduct that pampers to social needs; be the actor you have to be, like the cog in the machine, to facilitate harmony among the lab rats that you are. Because people are not shackled and whipped slaves in the modern office, when they are afforded the time and mental space, they can be different things depending on what they have to do. A call centre Muppet can be helpful, sadistic, or plainly inept. A manager can be funny, morose, or a workaholic. People can be almost anything they like until there is a dramatic conflict, which requires people to tactfully play their part: the fool, pacifist, dragon, princess or knight.

The fool, funnily enough, is self-explanatory. You are the fool. There is a problem. How could you possibly fix the problem when, office-idiot that you are, you have no brain? Because there is both a problem and a fool, people will generously try to educate the fool so the problem never ever happens again, ever. The fool may not be so self-assured, but at least they are still employed and the helper momentarily enjoys a giddy righteous high.

The pacifist enters forays with one directive – to end hostilities, encourage all parties concerned to drop their anger and embrace in a unifying pacific hug. This will atomise the room of all negative energies. This kills a roaring conflict in its prime. In the peace-making process the pacifist is fulfilling their little duty, and hopes to be looked upon as that special someone who wishes harm on no one. In fact, the pacifist is the most dangerous person in the office because by gaining so much trust and attention they will reach a critical-mass whereby trust becomes a commodity they will use for their own gain; otherwise acquiring it was a complete waste of time.

The dragon is the active and ambitious monster that must step into a conflict and lay down the law, regardless of their intelligence, position, knowledge and foresight of the situation, and regardless of whether anyone actually wants their opinion. If you're facing a dragon, let it breath enough fire that it will have to gasp for air, retire to its lair, and re-fuel. If you have to play the dragon don't play about with kid-gloves: take a big breath and scream down peoples' necks. Although you may be infringing on the code of civility, you are giving people guidance, a sense of order, and they are taking orders from you. And the dragon can always be blamed later. Dragons don't mind blame either – they have thick skin.

The princess is not simply the 'bright-eyed, bushy-tailed, young-thing' flirting her way through the office to cover of the tracks of her silly mistakes. The princess is the one who needs to be rescued, and like the fool, how can they be blamed for being what they are? People, (fools that they are) like to rescue the princess from situations by intervening and playing the charming knight. Playing the knight is chivalrous, yet true knights never rescue an annoying princess twice, and if they do they face a role reversal – knight becomes fool.

Burying the Dead – Hiding the Evidence

To dispose of a body in the office is extremely difficult – rotting flesh easily spoils the serenity and sterility of an air-conditioned environment. Therefore, it's not advisable to dispose of bodies in the workplace unless an air-tight lockable room can be found, which you are sure no one uses. Archive rooms, the basement, and stairwells fall in this category but they are also frequented by workplace lovers.

For document destruction there is always the trusty paper shredder. To ruin a printed document that must be filed for 'safe-keeping', spill something on it; coffee is not enough, try something really creamy so that in time, bacteria will multiply and the document will smell. Who would dare keep it? Surely it's backed-up on a hard-drive *somewhere*.

Thanks to the digital age, accountability, a few nutty terrorists and the ensuing climate of fear, as well as obsessive data-mining, your output on a keyboard is kept indefinitely. Therefore, to propose something using an electronic platform you must camouflage your true intentions with a specific code: nearly all industry leaders have a particular jargon relevant to the time and context to describe what they are going to do. It is only later, when the jargon has filtered through to the bottom of the knowledge food chain that people understand what is going on, and yes, by then it is too late.

Short of speaking gibberish, the best way to hide evidence is to keep it as an idea for as long as possible. Shape it in your mind, and when you are ready relay the idea to like-minded fellows or the computer. Unleash your idea but beware of technology, you can try to hide or alter it, but information technology professionals, if called in at the right price, can make up whatever *they* want. Make your evidence obscure – mention something broad when about to perform something exact, and vice versa. Save yourself the hassle of burying evidence by creating less of it.

Stealing Ideas

Number One – Don't be afraid.

Number Two – Don't get caught.

Number Three – If you do, take charge of the situation, and carry the idea forward into action.

Number Four – If it all leads to failure, remind everyone it was never your idea.

This is how things work. As a matter of fact, it is so ingrained in society and is not only tolerated but expected, because the majority of people who actively steal ideas and take responsibility are the ones who risk turning an idea into an eventuality or a stinking fat failure. If you have an idea, move forward with it, even pass it on to someone more capable. Let them carry it and if they take the glory, and if it angers you, give them another great idea. Let them take this, let them run away and when they come back to you for another idea, hold your own ground. Make demands. If you really had a very good idea, don't worry, there will be more.

If your idea is stolen and success is the outcome for someone wholly undeserving, get over it. Yes, plot a cold revenge, but move on. The thief will never ever admit to the theft, so give them another idea – a poisoned idea. Now watch them play their usual games and fall in a trap. Plan your exit or even better, plan a fat profit from their downfall.

Spies

Get into your mind the scenario that you are already a spy (primarily for yourself), and that you are inadvertently spied upon by everyone else. People feed off what you radiate – spies seize upon scraps of information haphazardly thrown away. They scuttle away and report to their master. To turn someone into a spy you must unite them in a cause. Naturally, friends can be trusted and enemies certainly not. Rivals can be spies, because one rival may be coerced into helping you to get them ahead of all the other rivals. Yes, a time will come when this brief alliance will fall apart, but in the meantime your exchange of information will accelerate both of you to a higher ground.

Nearly anyone can be incorporated into your spy network, but if you pay too much attention to what everyone says, then you will have an omnipresent spy network that feeds you nothing but rubbish. If you are known to use spies, then those against you will corrupt your spies into double agents. It is better to recruit someone as your spy who is passive but with little ambition, and who craves some excitement to make their dreary life seem worthwhile. Do not tell them exactly what they are to you; create a relationship based on a mutual interest. Do not immediately ask them questions that would arouse suspicion. Be patient with spies, and above all reward them.

Accountability and Deflecting Blame

For some, the art of deflecting blame is their only *strategy*. Their tactics are focussed on existing, and never being accountable for anything unless the outcome is fruitful and positive so they receive the reward. For the average knowledge warrior, deflecting blame is an escape mechanism adapted according to the situation and how honourable they feel at the time. There are two reasons to deflect blame: One, it is not your fault. Two, it is your fault but you wish it weren't. Regardless of the reason, the outcome is to be the same: Someone else is to blame. Entire industries are built on deflecting blame, shifting accountability, proclaiming innocence, and carrying out due-diligence to prove they could never be to blame for something they might be blamed for in the future. At a basic level, you should know before you are involved in anything, the risk, reward and the probability that people will blame you, first and foremost, if there is a problem. Don't play pool with professional hustlers and don't work with professional blamers.

People deflect blame by removing themselves from the inception, implementation, ownership, outcome, and anything else they can think of when the shit hits the fan. There is no end to deflecting blame and the more a person grasps for reasons why they are not to blame, the more they are to blame. The energy people spend deflecting blame could be used correcting simple mistakes, but people are scared of having one mistake ruin their career and thwarting their path to power, glory, and riches. Can you blame them?

If you wish to be a success in the world, promise everything, deliver nothing – Napoleon Bonaparte

Admitting Mistakes

Do not be afraid to admit mistakes, because honesty is valued. Do be afraid to admit other peoples' mistakes because stupidity and duplicity is *not* valued. The greatest advantage to admitting mistakes, taking blame, showing accountability, is that the knowledge gained is primarily yours. You know why something went wrong, not just in theory but in practice. Your knowledge can be called upon in other areas to make sure other people don't fuck up like you did, and in the process, you earn your redemption. On the other hand, your reputation for failure may precede you, so you might be valued for your ability to screw things up – see 'Serial Incompetence'.

Acknowledging All As Known – Fake Genius

The art of knowing everything is showing no surprise when hearing new information. If a messenger is telling you something new and surprising, just nod sagely, maintain eye contact with the messenger and change subject just when you have heard enough to fit the remainder of the information together yourself. Never explain how you come to know so much (without being a know-it-all) but do proclaim to have warm, close contacts with all the knowledge chiefs in the organisation. This fools the majority until a select few suspect your trait and will bait you into knowing things that never were, or if you did know them, could have saved the organisation at some point from a mini-disaster. In this situation, you must deny.

Denying Knowledge You Never Knew

This is easy: you never knew it, and if found that you did when you didn't, you can easily claim confusion from information overload or that information was mixed up with another subject. The next step is to ask someone else for a lengthier and more concrete explanation.

> *The best way to keep one's word is not to give it*
> *– Napoleon Bonaparte*

Denying Denying Denying^{Denying}

In some offices denial is a code of conduct. People talk about anything other than the "one important issue", because it puts off the inevitability of having to deny something even when nothing had been said about the issue. This is a frightful Kafkaesque situation, but it is a reality. People deny things before they know what they're denying; to save denying *denying*. It appears that only the deniers survive, because when you have a group of deniers (a united faction) and someone (an individual of the moment) who doesn't deny, the latter will be ostracised – not for being honest – but because the sum total of the deniers' 'guilt' will pour out. This response is not out of gratitude for the individual's mistake for telling the truth, but in scorn because their lies may be unravelled. The odd one out is singled out for undue ridicule. When swimming with shark-minded deniers, remember one rule: denying is lying, and lies create more lies, which is what becomes the denier's undoing.

At some point they have to admit to denying, but when you call a spade a spade, they'll deny denying denying.

Magic Numbers = Statistics

We can add, subtract, multiply, and square-root numbers in our minds or utilise the calculators embedded in our computers, mobile phones, and toothbrushes. We can let technology do the hard work for us. We can play all night with numbers and be fascinated by their simplistic beauty. But when someone does it for us and arranges them into a statement, a diagram based on statistics – the truth and nothing but the truth – why do we recoil for fear of impending doom, or salivate in a fit of gluttony – depending on what the diagram is programmed to make us feel? Be aware that anytime anyone shows you statistics, no matter in what form they take (data, reports, graphics or surveys, for example) remember that before they compiled the holy statistics, they had a holier directive to abide by. They are obliged to please their patron, and what their patron doesn't like in the raw data will be changed to suit their strategic objective.

Statistics are used much like a drunk uses a lamppost: for support, not illumination – Vin Scully

Deception, Hot Air, Smoke and Mirrors

Magicians are paid to deceive. Their sleight of hand, smoke and mirrors, orchestrated darkness, and our amazement at their tricks, are all part of the routine. We happily pay for it, just as we vote in lying politicians.

Magic happens in the same way in offices. The deceiver has something to hide so they resort to a simple trick – create a diversion. They raise an issue to a level of severe importance. They coerce and include those stupid enough into a rescue mission; they lead the mission on an adventure which ends with a big finale whereby all involved feel a sense of achievement. Meanwhile, the deceiver has buried the bodies of those they killed, washed their hands of their corporate mistakes, and deleted all evidence, while they staged an entertaining spectacle to prevent people snooping around.

The best way to see through a deception is to ask: is it necessary? If it's happening this week, why didn't it happen last year? Once you spot a deception, find out what there is to conceal. What was the deceiver so anxious about before? Once you find out what the deceiver never wants anyone to know, you can bring them under your control.

Exit Strategies

We all have one, and when locked you are locked in a conflict, permit your opponent one. In so doing, you are not demonstrating benevolence, gratitude or a saving grace; you are basically avoiding a final confrontation that may get very, very bloody. A cornered animal fights to the death, so once you have cornered someone and made it clear that, for example, their job is in your hands, let them break out to begin a new job somewhere else. The entire application and interview process for jobseekers is a series of hoops to jump through, so prospective employees get to re-invent and re-write their employment history, strengths and weaknesses, and the big whopper of an excuse why left their last job.

If you have to make a hasty exit you have two options:

1. You wish to exit and return; therefore you conform to the office code of civil conduct. Make excuses that deflect blame, or take blame and turn it into something you can learn from. And above all, be noble.

2. If you are to exit and never return, (and this includes not requiring a reference), have some fun and tell people what you really think. The nastier you are, the higher the chance they'll invite you back and pay you double.

If it's not a matter of losing jobs, and you do give someone a point of exit from a conflict, you will witness their feigned apology. Their excuse will A) exonerate you and B) highlight one of their little mistakes, which is ostensibly an un-official cessation of conflict. If you allow someone an easy exit and they spit on your gratitude, you should pounce on them and bring them into line.

Downsizing

Is downsizing socially responsible? Who cares? What is downsizing? Is it competitive restructuring, that reduces labour costs by culling the average (and less than average) performing drones, or by ousting the expensive star performers? Is it true that downsizing does not result in an improvement in profits, because there are hidden costs in downsizing? Is downsizing really what it says on the can? Is it misconstrued by both parties when an owner just wants to fire the disgruntled, troublesome, and expensive employees in the name of economic rationalism? Or is it absolutely necessary, otherwise the business goes to the wall, and the sad sacked employees have a 'safe' excuse to give at their next job interview when asked why they left their last job?

In dizzying anti-communicative corporate environs, no one except the leaders of the racket at the very top, know what's going on. Downsizing could easily be called 'experimenting', 'ditching the trouble-makers/dead-weights', 'preparing for the worst', 'juggling employees because we're all corporate performers' or 'it's all the rage – let's just downsize'. Downsizing is an excuse when the truth won't do. If you face the prospect of being downsized, recognise that it's a perfect excuse to cover up what really went on. So, in effect, downsizing is part of a cosy deal, whereby all that can be said is, "There was a fuck-up. I had nothing to do with it. Someone employee me, please."

There's nothing wrong with being fired – Ted Turner

Outsourcing

Like downsizing, there is no need to take outsourcing personally. If you're staring down the barrel of being outsourced, it's because somewhere, (either the other side of the world in a developing country or just down the road in a developing business), someone will do your job for less. This is not much different from how you'll shop around before buying something expensive. Labour can come at a discount, even a significant discount. Feel better?

If you do feel better, you are easily fooled.

If you don't, you are waking up to a reality. Being outsourced (not you, your means of making money) feels like being abandoned, so you will experience the usual feelings: denial, surprise, anger – much like a teenage break-up. It's not so bad, but it is. The next thing to do, like the broken-hearted teenager, is to move on, preferably into a role that can't be outsourced.

Whatever cushy job you have in the West is coveted by the rest
– Simon Drake

The Interview

The interview is a contest for a job – they have it and you want it – or so it seems. But interviews can be many things.

- ✦ An organisation may hold interviews to examine the 'talent' out there, and to determine how desperate they are to leave their current job for the advertised position. This tells the organisation that the 'job' – real or not – should have a higher or lower remuneration package, be expanded or diversified, or even shelved.

- ✦ Some interviews are formalities. A successful candidate has already been chosen (internally, or through referral), but interviews are held to show to the public (as well as those internally that tried and never had a chance) that the job is open to anyone. These interviews are dull affairs, because try as they might, the candidate can't get the job, and the interviewer can't truly get excited about tormenting or tempting them about it.

- ✦ Candidates can be fakes. They may be doing the rounds, punching above their weight, going to interviews for jobs they'll never get (because their resume is a succession of lies), perhaps because they love talking about themselves for an hour and can't afford therapy. They may also believe that one day they'll 'wing it', and get a job they don't deserve – which happens all the time funnily enough.

Let us suppose the interview, job, and candidate are real. In this scenario there are four variations of interviews:

	Interviewer	Candidate
Interview Variation 1	Lying	Lying
Interview Variation 2	Lying	Honest
Interview Variation 3	Honest	Lying
Interview Variation 4	Honest	Honest

Candidates lie to the same degree that an interviewer will lie about the job on offer, so an interview may evolve through all four variations and still lead nowhere. But if a job has to be filled a fool has to be found. Anything can happen. Even if there is a pact of truthfulness by both parties, there still remains the X factor – who is to be chosen. When the right person is chosen, the interview process has been a success. When there are ten right people and one is chosen for some abstract reason – an oddball reason inevitably comes into the selection process somewhere – the interview process is an outstanding success. If the nine failures lie awake at night pondering a thousand and one 'If only I'd said...' scenarios then they are fooling themselves.

The truth is: success in interviews can be pure luck.

Interviews are half a slotting of experience, personality and skills into a position and half an evaluation by the interviewer whether they like you or not. Human Resources staff, gate-keepers to many an organisations' ranks, have specific systems to sort what is what and what it is for – you can lie as much as you want about your attributes, but if you haven't got the required skills, experience, age, white-teeth or short skirt – go home. And even if you do, and you're not on their wavelength and thus deemed 'not one of us' – go home, come back as a contractor and bill them twice as much as a wage slave.

So, what would you describe as one of your weaknessess?

Well, when it comes to interviews, bitches like you.

The Discrimination Card

Wednesday morning office warfare is going along fine and dandy: three idiots are battling it out over God knows what, using all their favourite rehearsed cliché one-liners – artful vernacular swipes at exposed intellectual jugulars. And then someone from the sideline asks, "Is that person being discriminated against?" All of a sudden the conflict erodes like sandcastles into the sea. Was there really discrimination? Now it may become a battle of 'if there ever was', or 'definitely wasn't'. Enter on the stage, the show stealer, Guilt.

Confrontation on a level playing field, with a hint of honour to spice up the drab corporate fanfare, should be fought by individuals with only their wit and intelligence. But when the battle turns into a 'you don't respect me because I'm [insert your preferred weapon of mass discrimination]!' spat, things have turned very nasty, and sadly, desperate.

Some play the discrimination card to upset their foe; anti-discriminatory rhetoric is so deeply embedded in Western institutions that to even think you may have inadvertently made a Freudian slip or chosen the wrong descriptor for a person – thereby exposing your inner-demon-discriminatory-self – can send the best of us into years of pious self-examination. After all, deep down, everyone has a discriminatory view on something.

The discrimination card does protect people; particularly those who feel vulnerable to discrimination. But most people who can easily be discriminated against don't pull the discrimination card at all. To use it makes them feel cheap, and sends a message that they are dangerous to their colleagues when it comes to confrontation, and so they are unable to have an intelligent argument ever again! How drab life can be for the discriminated.

When all is said and done, there will always be discrimination and reverse-discrimination, and even though it is legally outlawed on one level, it will be played out on another, proving that the law, like people, is not perfect.

Unleash the Arsehole or the Angel in You

It's OK to be an arsehole. Humanity is packed with arseholes, some of them famous, but 99.999% stuck in obscurity. The modern office is the one place in the world where you can feel comfortable being an arsehole, because you're getting paid and maybe even promoted, on a results basis. Often the more you frustrate people, the further you go – naturally this is relative to what other skills you have – but because you're an arsehole – your skills are lies anyway.

The most misunderstood aspect of being an arsehole is that you might not be a real one. You may in fact be doing something necessary, but other people will think of you as an arsehole because it interferes with what they want. Take time to consider what they are saying, perhaps for a nanosecond then get on with what you have to do. It's a jungle out there.

The angel in you is the inverse of the arsehole, and yes it is all in the eye of the beholder (or arsehole). True angels do not perform acts of goodness with the crushing piety of benevolence in mind; they do it as a shark chomps on fish all day – pure automata. Alas, angels do not seek reward, so you can't pay them appropriately, or be paid yourself.

Hatred is gained as much by good works as by evil
– Niccolo Machiavelli

The Battle of the Sexes

One day humanity will utilise technology to morph itself into transient and sexless beings that roam the cosmos awaiting the demise of the universe. Mankind and womankind will be extinct. We will all wear short skirts and piss standing up. But until this spooky epoch, there will be issues of inequality, resistance from both sides, idealists trying to close the big gender divide, all to the tune of the usual sing-song of cries of discrimination and reverse discrimination. As glass ceilings for career women are removed, times change yet reality doesn't: men face glass ceilings as well.

There really is no end to it: men and women are different. There are workable possibilities for placing a man in a woman's job and a woman in a man's job, but it must be noted that it's always a competition for the good jobs anyway, and genders instinctively close ranks if they feel their point of peculiarity and superiority is at threat. These initial hostile feelings can be transformed into acceptance, and then it's the norm to have a man in a woman's job, a woman in a man's job, and there's no problem at all really. All it takes is time, mutual understanding, and the threat of a fat lawsuit.

The Battle for the Sex

We are all programmed to have a good time and it's only the moral codes laid down by the righteous and wise that stop us from slipping into a barbaric orgy of sin, fun, and debauchery. In (short) skirts, shirts and ties, we appear well behaved eight hours a day, disciplined, professional, humble, cohesive, together. But on the inside we crave rivalry, a good time, deep penetration, and though we can't hold hands, skip down the hallway, strip and spread ourselves over the boardroom table physically, we do it mentally. There are thousands of little games going on. The releasing of flirtatious desires could lead to a night in a cheap hotel with expensive champagne, but the most gratitude you'll probably receive is the battering of the eyelids from someone you fancy, and now you know, fancies you – without the love children, home-breaking and general uproar. These are the little score points in life that we tally at the end of the day and prize more than the percentage points of productivity and duplicity to the machine we slave for.

We are all blessed with a certain sexiness, which, if used wisely, can help us up the ladder (or keep us on it), and everyone uses what they've got. Even those who are not so aesthetically pleasing to the eye will utilise some subtle sexual power to get their way; they might use humour, know how to have a good time, but be a real bitch/bastard.

For most individuals, it is a question of preference as to how you play your sex appeal, and there's not a great deal you can do to alter yourself, you are what you are. No matter how hard you try to shape your sexual prowess and destiny into a weapon or shield, there's limited scope for action because it's all in the audience's perception. There's fashion to sex you up or down, but pheromones, age, wellbeing, mood and countless other factors render you either attractive or repulsive. We cannot be sexual tigers all the time.

Therefore there is a demand for people with obvious sexual traits. A competitive office landscape can be further excited up by hiring some high-calibre, high-class, eye-candy to perk the team up. Or, for the opposite effect, hire an old saggy thing to dampen things down. It all depends on what those in charge want and are willing to pay for, and accept; which might be beauty over brains. Perhaps they just want a stereotypical nerdy brainiac to tinker with the computers, so as not to distract the bored girls (or the gay guys) in the typing pool and marketing department.

Using sex, whether it be innuendo or even the act, is handy for some and it may take them all or some of the way. But for most people sex is fun, free, usually safe, and kept away from the office desk, safely in bed, or the woods.

The Battle Within the Sexes

Battles within genders for sexual superiority claim more casualties and wastes more time than male vs. female feuds over equality and preference, but is also a buzzing energy not to be wasted. Divisions within genders based on looks, brains, strengths, and status are sources of contention, and because they create feuds and rivalry (think of all the bitches and bullies out there jostling for prime position on their little imaginary hierarchies) they let off natural steam and create good competition. It is a resource not to be wasted, although it can easily cause waste – two people of the same gender trying to prove their higher status can cause collateral damage. As in the context of the savagery of nature, there has to be a decider. It's only natural for someone to want to be the most manly or the most womanly, at the top of their gender pyramid, even if they're not in any position of real power in the organisation. How they get there is by establishing a commitment to the job, proving their professional traits, and having the brightest lipstick or smelliest armpits. Once they've established their social role amongst their gender, the others can relax; the feuding over sexual superiority is over and we can all get back to mundane things, like office work.

Pro-Active Persuasion:
Brown-Nosing & Begging

Because we are obliged to do a number of required (and some ancillary) tasks for an income, our methods of persuasion in the office stretch far beyond what we would normally do in any other situation. You don't greet your annoying relative the same way you do your annoying manager, even though both may cause you the same grief and restless nights trapped in a quandary as to how to handle them.

Concentrate on the manager or anyone else who has power over you. Take away the promises of job security, promotion, a raise, a stronger sense of purpose and all that chaff. In a flash all the charming persuasive body language and harks of commendation in the office disappear. But wake up! You're in a competitive environment and like everyone else, pro-actively persuading to get what you want.

You might think that how you conduct yourself should get you what you want, but whether you like it or not, pro-active persuasion, grovelling, choreographed begging, and performing some face saving flip when cornered by a nasty character is what's really required. It's also a signal to you and all concerned that it's your last resort. Every other tactic failed, so you're reduced to this.

When in this position, remember that because you couldn't get what you wanted before, you have to step out of yourself and gleefully lick boots, because your normal natural self has not enabled you to get what you want. In the system you are in, you let you down. Therefore licking boots, brown-nosing, sucking-up, is humiliating, but it is also fortifying; your little mind will be planning how to never ever do this again. The owner of the boots you're licking may even feel a touch of compassion towards you, but on the other hand they may want a tonne of humiliation from you as proof that you're committed. Whether you are giving or receiving, never forget what it's about: gaining favour.

Regardless of who you are, you have to do it sooner or later; most probably to the type of person you despise the most. Be aware of people who can bow down easily and swiftly and unleash their grovelling to exonerate themselves, charm and subdue, and generally get what they want, whereas others mumble and cringe and dream of better things. Those that can brown-nose at the drop of a hat are nasty characters, not just because they'll expect the subservience they so freely gave to others to be returned, but because they are probably very good at getting what they want with minimal effort. Five minutes of solid brown-nosing to the right person can further their career more than five months of solid work tucked away in the corner of the office.

If you have to partake in pro-active persuasion, think ahead, plan the method, tie it to a strategy, and make it direct. Understand how and why other people do it. Is it defence or attack? Is it ritualistic and expected? Who are the players and what are their motives? Does it always work? When faced with a grovelling knowledge worker, do certain people kick sand in their face, or collapse like a spineless house of cards? A passive person has little need to please lots of people, so persuading the select few that hold the purse strings will suffice. An active person, warped by drive and ambition, will be honing their ways of persuasion on a daily basis – the goal is simple – to gain favour with those above, so they can manoeuvre into an advantageous position.

This is how the professionals do it:

- ✦ They manage a permanent state of agreement between themselves and those that matter. It's all positive, '100% understood agreement', yes-yes. Nothing is ever regarded as a problem, even disasters are seen as minor glitches, but when blame has to be apportioned, they will be the first to help those at the top adjust their aim.

- ✦ Their energy is focussed on the organisation's mantra. They know the codes of conduct. They make a show of boosting team spirit, acting as conduit towards the top, playing the vital pillar of support. All this is of course a disguise – they may in fact be a subversive team-wrecker, but on the outside they are shining to those above; they are a prime example of what to be and how good all should always be. Think: golden child.

♦ They don't make public enemies, and conflict is carried out on their terms, well away from spectators and speculators. But they are quickly transmitting their concerns in the nicest possible manner to those above. They don't just CC emails, they BCC.

♦ Their methods of persuasion extend from superfluously congratulatory language to readily identifiable body language and transformations that are geared towards those they're performing for. They mimic those above, because after all their aim is to stand shoulder-to-shoulder with them. An easy parallel is to watch a group a chimps: the subordinates obey the alpha, mimic movements and walks, but when they get too perfect the alpha comes down on them. When the professional arse-licker has to belittle someone, they'll do it with a gentle, sterile finesse, all by the book. And it hurts.

♦ There are no set rules to pro-active persuasion. There is no code of conduct either. Professionals use whatever they have (e.g., high heels, macho profile, bitchy attitude, or the merits of their expensive education or hard-done-by-life proudly pinned to their chests) to sow their seeds, water their ideas, and shape the outcome to their gain. Professionals don't hold back, and if they are called to account they will deny everything and arse-lick their way out of trouble.

All this pro-active persuasion from dunces and professionals is fine and dandy, but it can't go on indefinitely. It a sign that you've tried everything else and now you have to lick some boots. The recipient must signal at some point that your begging has been heard and we can all move on. The surest way to get your message across is for them to show they have the upper hand. A conversation might end with 'Yes you will do that', or something else painfully obvious. If it's body language, watch for the classic interlocked fingers, hands on the crown or at the back of the head, arms wide, back stretched, and underarms exposed to the poor arse-licker. It may be painful to look at but it's the sign that the arse-licking is over for now.

Combating Pro-Active Persuasion

At the heart of the pro-active persuasion is righteous politeness ('I'm trying to do my best for the best of the rest'), and as politeness and righteousness are two variables, just as beauty is all in the eye of the beholder, once displayed they can be used as points to work against.

When combating an ardent arse-licker, be sure to do it right in their face, using what they think is their little superiority. Take a stand on what they take on stand on. Breath some fire and make them run for cover. Be forceful, because arse-lickers like things done subliminally, by *their* flowery coercion.

If faced with excessive politeness, and you decide to use extra politeness to get your way, things can lead to politeness overload. But this can't last forever, because someone will lose their calm façade and crack; hopefully it is not you. Remember that politeness requires an audience, and as the audience is there to be won over, politeness sinks into entertainment. Make a case, attach it to a story, and turn your competitor into the villain.

If your competitor is a ruthless arse-licking liar, who operates according to the socially acceptable rules of the office, and they get their way and block your way, put on a brave face. Their ruthlessness, as forceful and deceitful as it is, is an anchored weakness. People may be wary of the ruthless arse-licking liar but understand that there is a ratio: the more frequently ruthless someone is, the more their ruthlessness becomes ineffective. Bait them into a public discussion, force an argument, get their temper up and watch the audience's abhorrence at the arse-licker's ruthless and childish behaviour. This approach is quickly thrown out the window if person you're dealing with is also in a position of un-assailable power. This is a worse cast scenario, and yes, to combat them, spread gossip whenever possible, lay the knife in their back, mastermind the eroding of their powerbase, and act extra-pleasant all the while. Make their downfall your pet, spiteful project.

Do Nothing

There is so much going on in the office, so many plans and thwarting of plans, thinking and masterminding, deduction and suspicion. Everyone is up to something. Yet one of the most amazing tactics is one that few come up with when devising and orchestrating their nasty plans – do nothing. 'Doing nothing' is not a mindless, apathetic, or slovenly choice that springs to mind – it's an educated move, based on assessing the drawbacks of doing something, or doing exactly what your opponent wants you to do.

To 'do nothing' after careful consideration enables you to keep an ace up your sleeve. Withhold what you can until the last minute and then strike. If the shit hits the fan, don't get anxious when time is on your side.

Be Nice and Be Wise

When all is said and done, when all cunning aspirations are cast aside, all we want to do is to be nice. Yes there are contradictions in being nice, but it's good to be nice because you can and good things will come of it. Being nice should be a default until someone comes to use your niceness for their own gain. Here's when you have to be wise. The assertiveness that follows can be nice as well, after all to break your good run of niceness because of a few bad apples is no way to live a nice life. Don't let people upset your inner calm, and if they do, it's wise to retaliate with lots of force. In order to be truly nice, it's wise not to take shit from anyone.

I never think of the future. It comes soon enough
– Albert Einstein

Art of Office Communication

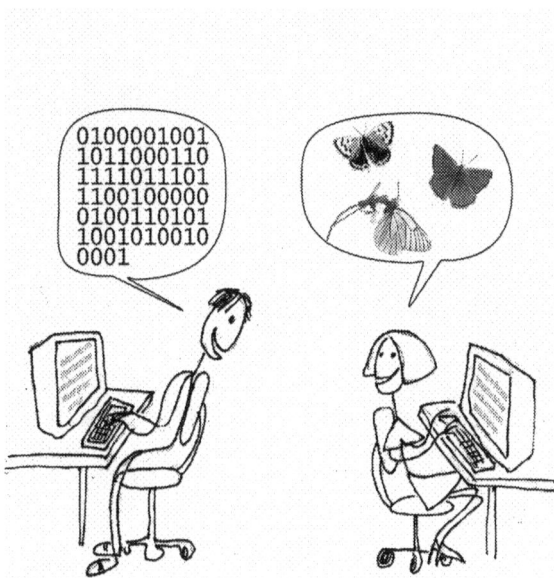

Money for Words

Communication isn't just about touching a button and chairing a video conference call between two research stations in sub-zero temperatures at different poles of the earth. Communication is a loop of hearing, comprehending and replying. Good communication skills involve speaking less and rationally evaluating what you hear. So why are there so many communication problems in the office? Is it perhaps, intentional? Or purely accidental and occupational? Why don't we get sick of hearing the same old stuff? Is it because we get paid for it?

> *A dog is not considered a good dog because he is a good barker.*
> *A man is not considered a good man because he is a good talker*
> *– Buddha*

Lack of Communication

Do not confuse non-communication as a lack of communication. Lack of communication can involve several people conversing about something not related to what they should be talking about, because they are too afraid of expressing individualistic views. To avoid lack of communication, separate people and talk to them individually. Comfort them, trick them, do anything to avoid lack of communication.

To enforce a lack of communication, to avoid an issue (usually one of your outstanding career-threatening mistakes) get everyone talking and excited about anything and command them accordingly. Politics is strife with 'lack of communication', because political beings are constantly kicking more flavoursome issues into the air for the benefit of the crowd, and as we know crowds and society in general love a spectacle. So the more sizzle the better, without ever having to feed the masses with the raw, cold, disgusting sausages.

Gossip and Miscommunication

Gossip is information based on personal and third party observation, embellished with emotional critique. The majority of gossip *is* fiction; factional or individual. But sieved gossip can deliver vital intelligence if the emotional twist is rinsed away by harsh perception. In fact, by listening to gossip and hearing the gist of the story tells more about the person telling it than the subject; a weakness, or perhaps their strength to talk at all, is a useful tool, but do not misconstrue the fact that you are hearing it as an element of trust. Gossip requires little drive, energy, and direction. It is plainly there no matter what's going on.

> *Everything we hear is an opinion, not a fact.*
> *Everything we see is a perspective, not the truth*
> *– Marcus Aurelius*

Strategic Communication

The most important communication is the hardest to find. When people say what they mean they do it in confidence. However, to receive this strategic communication second-hand may be misleading. What is said to one means something different to another. Therefore, for the best strategic communication, speak to the appropriate person and no one else. Don't waste time asking the wrong people – unless of course you want to waste time in search of a loaded answer (which is an excellent way to mislead people from finding out something you want kept secret). Naturally, you have to gain trust for strategic information, but you can also coax it out of people in an argument, perhaps by letting them have the last point over you. People love drama, they love to prove a point, and if it is dear to their heart they need to be coerced into excommunicating it.

Information Overload

In the office there is an abundance of stimulating information. Even the gentle hum of the photocopier is a source of inspiration (someone is employed to do the photocopying, and you may be demoted/promoted to that position). There is also the natter of staff: gossiping, talking to friends on the phone, typing emails, talking to themselves, talking to you about *you* talking to yourself. Then there are memorandums, newsletters, reminders, an avalanche of arse-saving echo communiqués that have one specific purpose: saving someone from blame or ridicule should something fuck-up. Most importantly there are vital bits of information, such as what your manager is saying and not saying, bits and bytes about how you need to prove your worth. Add to that the intensity of the western world: every single day we are shovelled advertisements, news updates, scraps of other peoples' messages, feelings, emotions, across a wide range of delivery systems; human interaction, telephone, print and electronic media, and in some cases, experimental telepathy from God knows who. There is so much stimuli out there trying to tantalize your senses into making you believe something irrelevant and tax your wealth and time and deplete your personal gain. From a cave-man perspective, digging for worms, developing an innate sense of weather patterns, and finding healthy berries by trial and error, provided ample stimulation. After all, if you weren't stimulating yourself everyday on the savannah, you were probably starving, and, as Darwin noted, you wouldn't be around today. As it stands, unless you stripped naked and join the savages in the remotest jungles, you are stuck in the modern world. We are joined together, our economies and industries are inseparable, and your livelihood relies on a culture burdened by information overload.

But information overload clouds your senses and disrupts your rhythm. When you observe all that is happening with your eyes and ears you will be looking for links between all this stimuli. You will begin to draw conclusions and sort them for revelations. Absorb information because it is there, but do not try to formulate a series of conclusions and revelations to give you an edge. Let information overload flood over you and be absorbed, but passively. Let your subconscious trawl through the slush and let it feed your instinct. Trust your natural feelings, not the neatly packaged glittering bullshit served up as 'wisdom' by marketing gimmicks or a rival out to poison your mind. Quietly observe and be the master of your mind and all around you.

I have not told half of what I saw – Marco Polo

Email Communication

Email is a new invention but the software in our minds is not.

For tens of thousands of years we have been saying, 'Tell so-and-so this, but don't tell them-over-there, and tell me when so-and-so knows, and if you find out they and them-over-there are talking about me, tell me. And if I find out they're talking about you, I'll tell you, and we won't tell them, even if they ask, you got it?'

The only improvement with email is that with a single click, a piece of communication is sent TO: CC: BCC, or all of the above in milliseconds. The instantaneous nature of email is its weakness, "What have I just said?"

Write shorter and more precise emails to less and less people. Your goal is that when someone receives your email they will compare it with others and say, 'This person hardly ever sends email, so this must be important.'

However, if this dreary and perfunctorily state of minimalism annoys and bores you to tears – people saying only what is absolutely necessary and sucking dry the life of what should be vivid communiqués – retaliate by writing verbose tracts loaded with superfluous adjectives that seem out of place in a multinational, corporate, linear, context. Adopting the flair of a savant, and being 'radical' with the English language (or your own language) is perfectly legitimate. Strange as it may sound, it's refreshing to read what people really think.

The Loop and the Echo Chamber

The loop sounds great as a concept: communication goes around in a loop; everyone is in the loop, with equal access to information. We hear the same thing, and when we add something, it goes around the loop so we are all one and equal. But the term loop is synonymous with the echo chamber; we are all are in an echo chamber, and when people throw about ideas they come back to them just how they want them – they're all in there supporting others' points of view.

If someone is in the loop, it implies that other people are way out of it (mostly for good reason, but let's concentrate on servicing the loop and the echo chamber). If you have one, test it by throwing up an oddball proposition. Depending on your status, the majority will either support or slam it. If you are an important decision maker people will agree with your oddball proposition because in the confines of the loop and the echo chamber, people are frightened to say anything that contradicts what the knowledge chiefs say. For this reason, the loop and the echo chamber inevitably falls in on itself sooner or later. The key of course to a successful loop and echo chamber is to privately source strategic information.

Jargon

If you think jargon is a variety of zircon, a common mineral occurring in small crystals, the chief source of zirconium that is used as a refractory when it is opaque or a gem when transparent, then I love you. Before the digital age, another definition of jargon was: 'confused, unintelligible language; gibberish; hence, an artificial idiom or dialect'.

Thanks to the digital age, jargon is now defined as 'a specialized technical terminology characteristic of a particular subject'. In this time and era, people's livelihood depends on jargon, something which was once seen as completely senseless. So what is jargon? It is a name given to any subject by a select few to confuse the rest of us. As the digital revolution belched strings of binary into the sockets of PCs wired to the web, jargon became commonplace. Housewives have even been known to drop in jargon in passing conversations with their hairdressers, and if the other has no idea what it means, they simply nod and appear to agree by saying, 'Yeah... Totally', which is jargon in action, as it was originally defined. Jargon begets jargon.

Because jargon is used by a select few to describe their 'particular subject' in a compact form it serves them well: communication is the key to progress and they can tinker and chatter away in their own little secret language. Hopefully their invention will be a worthy contribution to humanity, understood one day by the masses, and only the necessary jargon (for an invention's operation) will filter down and be absorbed by the masses alongside all the other newfangled words of that era.

Jargon is also a weapon. The moment someone baffles you with jargon on a subject from their high ground, it may sound technologically convincing, but it is jargon in the truest sense; it is 'confused, unintelligible language; gibberish; hence, an artificial idiom or dialect'. This is many people's favoured means of averting your attention from their obvious deficiency. It is quite a joy to find someone's weakness, so don't pounce and tear them to shreds, wind them up that you believe them, take it all in, start talking their jargon back to them and they'll cling to you like a long lost friend. Now that you are friends, you can tell them truthfully that they don't know shit.

Deciphering the Endorsed Goodwill

Goodwill is exactly what it says on the label, "I mean goodwill."

So if you take the principle at its face value, don't be alarmed that as truth is the first casualty of war, goodwill is the cannon fodder, victim and culprit of any office struggle, "Well, we *meant* goodwill."

Goodwill is part of the utopian prospect of harmony, conjured up by professionals and served on a plate by master chefs to mask the true nature of something audacious and troubling. The moment goodwill is bandied about it, be wary because it appears as innocent as the sun's rays – it is there to promise the sun but blind us of reality.

Modern goodwill has become propaganda, engineered, and delivered according to the setting and desired outcome. As most outcomes for a corporation involve rewarding shareholders and those who bring in the bonuses, the setting involves abiding by of laws and making a legitimate profit, at the expense of dispelling the anxiety of the workforce that is chained to a wage and not much else. The projection of the notion of goodwill is simply to divert their minds. Very well, you are what you are, but as soon as goodwill is aimed straight at you – consider what they're really up to.

The Sweet & Sour of Political Correctness

Do not fear political correctness. Take your mind back to a far away time when we lived under one glorious Sun King and toiled away on his fields and built monuments to his glory. It was politically correct to communicate in a certain way that pleased the Sun King and his henchman, or we ended up as sacrifices, slaves or stationary archery practise, so we kept quiet and used irony to convey our inner dissatisfaction. Life went on.

Fast forward to the present. The 20th Century was punctuated by some very nasty acts (which will occur again sooner or later) and the civilised world arose from the ashes and decided, enforceable by laws, that all are equal. Post-war Western society was fortunate to have a giant lead in education so people in these societies, thanks to excessive time to be educated and excessive wealth to utilise the fruits of their studies, became enlightened (and some paid to) to a new state of thinking and enthralled in a new struggle and exploration: pushing the *wild* frontiers of *equality*. There have been good and bad consequences; just like old world explorers bashing exotic savages on the head with a bible and stealing their gold, those pushing the frontier of equality upon the many heathens out there require compensation for their effort of 'salvation' exerted. As the West is built on civility and equality (and not so much civility and equality to those not so in the West), the forcing of political correctness on the majority is vivid proof that all in the civilised world can be equalised (whether they like it or not), and if possible, just getting more equal than before.

Interpret the vogue of *über* political correctness like you would in former times – respect the Sun King or lose your head. Today, however, you respect the state's laws and play politically correct because it is the acknowledged means to impress, ally and above all, pacify, everyone and anyone, regardless of their peculiarity; anything that stands out from the average and could be used as a focus for possible discrimination. If you don't play the politically correct game, the worst case is that the state is there to enforce equality (by rewarding/compensating those treated un-equally) and punishing you, via a spectacle in a court of law; extracting wealth, privilege, and power from nasty little you. Political correctness protects (for many good reasons) legalised and legitimised minorities by annoying the majority (for which they can't fully understand the reason). As a means of extracting financial remuneration, the enforcement of political correctness is not far removed from Robin Hood's game of taxing those who pass through his forest. Robin Hood, however, isn't the same old bandit anymore and the forest, well it's now courts of law.

It pays to be politically correct in public, and self correct with yourself and those you trust. However, while playing political correct, remember that it is a game. You can play it safe and cautious, or you can play it to the extreme by inverting political correctness, so that it is shown as advantageous as jargon. Don't be afraid to add a fair portion of irony to your political correctness, because if the shit hits the fan and some righteous representative of the state's mighty laws doesn't like what you say, thanks to political correctness directives, your irony is your disability. Be proud of it. Wear it on your sleeve. Tell people it's not a behavioural problem, it is a personality enhancer. Give yourself the license to say what the fuck you want, when you want, or you will forever be muted and at the mercy of people who can communicate better than you.

Lying and Honesty

The biggest drawback to lying is having to create more lies to support the original lie. Simple lies are used to deflect invasive questions; complex lies have a strategy behind them, which is usually to do with discrediting something or someone, or even unduly promoting something or someone, through goodwill, or politically correct strategies. When someone says that something is better than something else, they are most probably lying. And one should always be able to understand why there are lies; people lie because they want something and the truth will not work for their cause. Many industries have information as their product, and use lies to sell their information – the lie becomes accepted yet not whole heartedly believed. This is an acceptable form of lying. If you believed they were telling the truth, then you would be a fool.

The biggest drawback to being honest is being honest again and again, even when people don't like what you're saying. You can be honest all your life, true to yourself and true to others, but do not forget that people like to be entertained. The greatest stories are a balance of honest accounts spiced with exaggeration. Because honesty and lying can blend so well and so appealingly, it is worth noting that having honest intentions the whole time, and being honest wherever possible, will carry you forward safely to where you want to go. There is no use arriving at your destination having followed the road of lies, and then having to answer for yourself.

> *When you want to fool the world, tell the truth*
> *– Otto von Bismarck*

Excuses

It's not the content of the excuse; it's the delivery that counts. 'Accountability', 'due diligence', and caution have a seemingly iron grip on people and organisations. People are petrified of mistakes, and when a mistake is made, there is an immediate creatively constructed trail of blame that leads to the least aware, or whomever the powers have chosen for a beating. Inevitably, there is an excuse. An excuse is the most artful form of escape, and needs to be mastered, but the act and delivery of the excuse is no simple matter.

The excuse must fit the context of the situation, and similar to proving a point, an excuse must disprove a point. An excuse, like a good joke, must also contain elements of surprise and timing because the recipient of the excuse wants to be entertained. And they probably foresaw that this was not going to be a straight apology; it was going to be a creepy excuse. The excuse has to be so entertaining that it spreads and is misconstrued, so that in time the excuse becomes folklore and the originator respected. In future you will be expected to make the grandest of excuses. Soon the doors of the Public Relations industry open to you.

The Empty Office Language

What does what mean, and how is it different from yesterday's definition? Why has the language of organisation, refined by thousands of years of progress and enlightenment, recently been castrated, censored, and streamlined into some generic, blandly conformist and painfully superfluous language, spiced with tasteless, clichéd, buzzed up, sexed up or down terms and confusing phrases? Is it to bore and confuse the whole for the benefit of the few, so that industry captains and government mandarins, by promoting such complicated languages, pretend to be transparent when nothing could be further from the truth? Has the empty office language become their High Ground and in comparison you can only speak with grunts and hoots? Or is this new language completely necessary to keep abreast of the complications and challenges of the changing world?

In short, if you can't beat them (or understand them), join them. It pays to learn the empty office language, because it gives you the ability to fit into the system, communicate anonymously, send, receive, reply, CC, BCC, and go to bed knowing that if you call in sick tomorrow, anyone can communicate like you do. For the empty office language, workers are interchangeable (provided they speak the lingo) and it is such an impersonal language (no matter how hard you try to add your eccentric twist into the jargon and gibberish it will be omitted by co-authors) that when you're not in the office, you have no part of it. This 'detachment' serves a purpose – in your work days you may be chained to the wheel but in your own time you are free to speak and read what the hell you like.

The End

Simon Drake
London
October 2006

www.ingramcontent.com/pod-product-compliance
Lightning Source LLC
Chambersburg PA
CBHW051835040426
42447CB00006B/546